LET IT ROCK

First published in Great Britain in 2014
by Soundcheck Books LLP, 88 Northchurch Road, London, N1 3NY.

Copyright © Neil Daniels 2014

ISBN: 978-0-9571442-8-6

All rights reserved. No part of this book may be reproduced or transmitted in any form or by any means, electronic or mechanical, including photocopying, recording, or any information storage and retrieval system without permission in writing from the publisher. This book is sold subject to the condition that it shall not, by way of trade or otherwise, be lent, resold, hired out or otherwise circulated without the publisher's prior consent in any form of binding or cover other than that in which it is published and without a similar condition being imposed on the subsequent purchaser.

Every effort has been made to contact copyright holders of photographic and other resource material used in this book. Some were unreachable. If they contact the publishers we will endeavour to credit them in reprints and future editions.

This title has not been prepared, approved or licenced by the management or members of Bon Jovi and is an unofficial book.

A CIP record for this book is available from the British Library

Book design: Benn Linfield (www.bennlinfield.com)

Printed by Bell & Bain Ltd, Glasgow

LET IT ROCK

THE MAKING OF BON JOVI'S *SLIPPERY WHEN WET*

BY
NEIL DANIELS

CONTENTS

FOREWORD BY PAUL SUTER vii

AUTHOR'S INTRODUCTION ix

IT HAPPENED IN 1986 xii

SELECTED TIMELINE (1986–1987) xv

PART ONE – SETTING THE SCENE

1. THE ENDURING APPEAL OF *SLIPPERY WHEN WET* 3

2. THE FIRST TWO BON JOVI ALBUMS 9

PART TWO – *SLIPPERY WHEN WET*

3. IN THE STUDIO 21

4. A SONG BY SONG REVIEW 30

5. THE COVER SLEEVE 39

6. THE REVIEWS & COMMERCIAL RECEPTION 44

7. THE *SLIPPERY WHEN WET* TOUR 50

8. REFLECTIONS ON *SLIPPERY WHEN WET* – WHAT THE ROCK WRITERS THINK 61

9. THE *SLIPPERY WHEN WET* TEAM 70

PART THREE – LIFE AFTER *SLIPPERY WHEN WET*

10. *NEW JERSEY* – THE ALBUM THAT FOLLOWED 77

11. FROM MELODIC HARD ROCK TO POP ROCK – BON JOVI IN THE PRESENT DAY 86

12. BACKSTAGE AREA – THOUGHTS & REMINISCENCES ON BON JOVI 95

PART FOUR – TOUR DATES & DISCOGRAPHY

THE *SLIPPERY WHEN WET* TOUR DATES 1986–1987   105

SELECTIVE DISCOGRAPHY – *SLIPPERY WHEN WET*   111

SELECTIVE DISCOGRAPHY – BON JOVI   114

SELECTIVE DISCOGRAPHY – SOLO WORK   124

AFTERWORD BY DEREK SHULMAN   127

BIBLIOGRAPHY & FURTHER READING   129

SOURCES   131

ACKNOWLEDGEMENTS   133

ABOUT THE AUTHOR   134

FOREWORD
BY PAUL SUTER

Way back in the halcyon daze of *Kerrang!* there were two parallel schools of thought amongst we writers; some of us got off on hanging out with our heroes, and some of us got off on finding heroes of the future, new bands that we were sure were going to change the world ... or at least make some really good albums and validate our predictions of success by being, er, successful.

One of my favourite sources was *Billboard* magazine, and to this day I still remember coming across a small piece on a new American band called Bon Jovi (thank God they changed their minds about calling the band Johnny Electric!), accompanied by a tiny, postage stamp sized photo of the band. As a trade publication, *Billboard* didn't deign to mention anything about the music itself, but that photo sure looked promising for any fan of US arena rock, they certainly had the look. So I picked up the phone and called PolyGram's international department and blagged a copy of said album, just being released in America but not even on the horizon in Britain.

Scanning my *Kerrang!* review now, it seems that I actually failed to predict massive, unrelenting, worldwide success, so dock me for prescience points. But, on the other hand, I did postulate that it was in the running for album of the year – it was January at the time – so I guess I can afford to be just a little bit smug.

I never actually met the band until *Slippery When Wet* and, to his eternal credit, Richie Sambora remembered that *Kerrang!* review and thanked me profusely for it. Pretty impressive to remember one journalist's name for nearly three years; what a genuinely nice man he is.

LET IT ROCK

That review of the debut album was just the first rave of many, and the record company climbed fully on board, putting the band on the road with much success in both America (opening for Scorpions) and Europe (opening for KISS), as well as a hugely successful Japanese debut. The momentum was enough to overcome the relative weakness of the second album, *7800° Fahrenheit*, which was a clear example of the old adage about having a lifetime to write your first album, and a lunchtime for the second, and it would go on to repeat the gold certification of the debut. But everyone knew that album number three was going to be critical if Bon Jovi were not to slip into a downward spiral.

And of course, as we all know now, *Slippery When Wet* was everything it needed to be, and more. In the hard rock genre, outsold only by *Back In Black* and *Led Zeppelin IV*, it has sold close to 30 million copies worldwide and represents a perfect storm of every element which goes to make a truly great record – songwriting, performance, production and engineering. Which is where we have to give due credit to the critical contribution of co-writer Desmond Child, recommended to them by Paul Stanley. To their credit, Jon Bon Jovi and Richie Sambora put their egos aside and welcomed his addition to the writing team, and would reap the rewards of his input when the new songs blew *Slippery When Wet* into the stratosphere.

The other critical additions to the team were Canadian producer Bruce Fairbairn and engineer Bob Rock – probably recruited on the basis of their excellent work with Loverboy – who played invaluable roles in shaping what the band brought to them in Vancouver into one of the finest records to ever emerge from the studio.

It's one thing to have great songs, but, as many can attest, it's another thing entirely to turn them into a great record, let alone a landmark album like this one.

Paul Suter
(Freelance writer & former *Kerrang!* journalist)

AUTHOR'S INTRODUCTION

Loathed by many, yet adored by many more, Bon Jovi are a success story: period. The critics have rarely been on their side, but when it comes to making commercial rock, they are kings; true rock Tsars. Many would argue that they have yet to better any of their first four albums, which are - at least in my opinion - fine representations of 1980s American melodic rock. Each has its own merits. But from *Keep The Faith* onwards, an album which brought a drastic change in sound and image, they have struggled to maintain credibility with "serious" rock fans; the kind of fans that crave more grit over gloss, the ones that want more guitars and stronger melodies. The debate continues as to whether Bon Jovi can in fact still be labelled "rock". However, that is a story for another time.

This book is an unashamed celebration of *Slippery When Wet*, not only their most successful album to date but also one of the most fun, toe-tappingly gleeful rock albums ever created. We might roll our eyes or pretend to yawn when we hear "Livin' On A Prayer" or "You Give Love A Bad Name" at a wedding, or when the karaoke king in the local pub belts out "Wanted Dead Or Alive", but when *Slippery When Wet* is played from start to finish it is, quite simply, joyous.

In these days of downloading single tunes or random shuffle plays on iPods, it is easy to overlook the basic running order of an album, its light and shade and its ebbs and flows. Much thought goes into the structure of an album and nowhere is this more apparent than on *Slippery When Wet*. From the grand opening organ notes of the intro to "Let It Rock" (known as "Pink Flamingos") to the New Jersey vignette that is "Wild In The Streets", the album takes the listener on a roller coaster ride worthy of an Atlantic City amusement park. If you haven't listened to the album from start to finish recently, as nature intended, do yourself a favour and you'll see the magnificence of the vision that the band and their team had. More to the point, it will take you back to a point in time where you first heard it and it will bring the memories flooding back. If you haven't had the pleasure of listening to it yet, I envy you – there is a treat in store for you.

O.K., so Bon Jovi might not be the deepest lyricists in the business, but that isn't their intention. And, as most music industry people will tell you, the lyrics are not as important as the melody when it comes to a hit song, though Bon Jovi sure know how to paint a picture. As musicians, they are severely underrated, but they know how to make a great tune and an even better chorus. Once they get those hooks into you, you're hooked and they don't let go. That's what they do, and they do it well. You would need a heart of stone for the sheer joy and exuberance not to rub off on you.

There are so many reasons why this album has been – and continues to be – so astronomically successful, but at its most basic, *Slippery When Wet* is the kind of album that you play and it makes you forget about any kind of troubles that you might have in your life, and it makes you want to aim for the Repeat button rather than Stop. Certainly, the talents of Desmond Child, Bruce Fairbairn and Bob Rock helped make it what it was and what it remains, along with the band members themselves.

This book sets the scene by offering a potted history of the band's first two albums, which preceded *Slippery When Wet*, before giving a history of the album itself. There are also detailed appendices which show where the band are today; the music they have made and how they triumphantly followed *Slippery When Wet* with the equally brilliant studio offering, *New Jersey*.

In some respects, this is a book that encapsulates a certain timeframe in Bon Jovi's career; perhaps a golden age. There are two sides to the band's career: before *Keep The Faith* and after. Although this book largely deals with the years before 1992's *Keep The Faith*, I elected to chronicle – albeit briefly – the mammoth selling follow up to *Slippery When Wet*, *New Jersey*, because they can be viewed as a pair considering that they have

AUTHOR'S INTRODUCTION

the same writing and production team, as well as a similar melodic rock blueprint. Also included in the appendices is a chronology of their music from *Keep The Faith* onwards, which serves to place *Slippery When Wet* in context. How does it stand up against their other albums? Why does it remain so special?

Sure, this is not a biography of Bon Jovi *per se*, but, to truly understand the power and appeal of *Slippery When Wet*, discussing the music that came before and after is vital to the story: nothing exists in a vacuum. This book is more than a "making of" type guide for fans. Indeed, hopefully, this little book could also act as a handy "fans' guide" to the band's career with a track by track review, current thoughts on the album from various well-established rock writers, as well as various other bits and pieces that are related directly (or indirectly) to the legacy of *Slippery When Wet*. Just why has this album had such an impact on millions of people around the world?

Also, to keep things on an objective level, I have included a lengthy and highly humorous piece on the album by *Classic Rock Revisited*'s Jeb Wright who, as you will later discover, is not a fan of the band. It makes for a more rounded book. Jeb's view on the album and the band is certainly passionate even though he doesn't rate either particularly highly ... or does he? Methinks the rock scribe doth protest too much! Nevertheless, I am a fan of the album hence this book. Hopefully, you will enjoy *Let It Rock*; it's written as a book that can be dipped in and out of at leisure and is perhaps a neat little reference book.

Slippery When Wet is one of the best mainstream American rock albums to come out of the 1980s ... in a blaze of glory.

Neil Daniels
www.neildanielsbooks.com

IT HAPPENED IN 1986

Do feel free to skip this bit if you were around at the time and don't want to remember, or if you weren't around and you aren't interested in the world into which Slippery When Wet *was born. I hope though it helps to paint a picture of the 1980s. 1986 had its fair share of tragic incidents, so bands like Bon Jovi helped lift the mood.*

The year started tragically with the *Challenger* Space Shuttle disaster, which killed all seven crew members including the first civilian astronaut Christa McAuliffe on 28 January. The take-off was broadcast live in TV and we shuddered as the horrors unfolded.

Space was much on our minds that year, with Halley's Comet paying a visit for the first time since 1910. In February it reached the nearest point to the Sun. Don't hold your breath for its next visit – it won't be back until 2061. The USSR launched the Mir Space Station too.

Over in Sweden, Prime Minister Olaf Palme was assassinated on 28 February after walking home from the cinema (hard to imagine the leaders of many countries walking anywhere in public). The crime remains unsolved to this day.

More tragedy with the Chernobyl nuclear power plant disaster in the Ukraine (then part of the USSR) in April. Traces of fall out were found in virtually every country in the Northern Hemisphere and the cancer rates in that area are sky high.

The same month, John McCarthy was kidnapped in Beirut and spent a long five years in captivity as retaliation for America's bombing of Libya on 15 April before his eventual release.

May saw *Hands Across America* where more than 5 million people formed a human chain from east to west coast to raise money against homelessness and hunger. In the same month Expo '86 – a world's fair – opened in Vancouver. From January to July, Bon Jovi were in the same city recording *Slippery When Wet.*

The second son of Queen Elizabeth II, Prince Andrew, married Sarah Ferguson at Westminster Abbey. The couple divorced in 1996. Neither of them have re-married, though both have remained in the public eye, particularly the ebullient Fergie!

Communist China first began dabbling in "informal" stock trading in August. They have never looked back. The London Stock Exchange meantime brought in computerized share dealing, which was known as the Big Bang. It certainly shook traders up.

Cargo ship *Khian Sea* left the US carrying 14,000 tons of toxic waste. It spent over a year looking for a home for the waste – Haiti drew the short straw.

Pan Am flight 73 was hijacked at Karachi airport in Pakistan by Abu Nidal terrorists. 20 of the 380 passengers were killed. The hijackers were caught and given life sentences in Pakistan.

Radio station WNBC's eye in the sky helicopter crashed into the Hudson River killing reporter Jane Dornacker on 22 October. In the same month, Britain's M25 motorway, an orbital ring road surrounding London, was opened. Due to the frequent traffic jams it is known as London's biggest car park.

The Iran-Contra affair first came to light in 1986. Illegal arms sales to Iran, it was hoped, would allow hostages to be freed, as well as allowing the funding of the Nicaraguan contras who wanted to overthrow the Sandinista government. This was against the Boland Amendment which sought to limit US intervention in Nicaragua. The Tower Commission was set up to investigate the matter and found that US President Ronald Reagan had no knowledge of the events.

LET IT ROCK

In football, Argentina lifted soccer's World Cup beating West Germany (as it was then) 3-2. In the UK, Liverpool FC clinched their first (and, to date, their only) league and FA Cup double by beating arch-rivals Everton 3-1 at Wembley. Although nobody knew it at the time, Manchester United's appointment of Aberdeen manager Alex Ferguson would see him at the helm of the club until 2013 as United went on to dominate English football.

In baseball, the Mets defeated the Red Sox in the World Series. In Superball XX, the Chicago Bears beat the New England Patriots 46-10.

At age 46, Jack Nicklaus was the oldest winner of golf's US Masters, whilst Mike Tyson's defeat of Trevor Berbick saw him, at only 20 years old, become the youngest world heavyweight champion in boxing.

West Tip won racing's Grand National and Alain Proust of France won the FIA Formula One World Championship.

Number one singles in the UK included The Housemartins' "Caravan Of Love" before they migrated into the Beautiful South, Chris De Burgh's evergreen "Lady In Red", Europe's Europop anthem "The Final Countdown", Billy Ocean's theme to the *Romancing The Stone* movie "When The Going Gets Tough" and Spitting Image's infuriatingly catchy "The Chicken Song".

The States meantime saw Lionel Richie hit top spot with "Say You, Say Me", Billy Ocean had hits both side of the ocean with "There'll Be Sad Songs (To Make You Cry)", Janet Jackson summed up the 1980s with "What Have You Done For Me Lately", as did Gwen Guthrie with "Ain't Nothin' Goin' On But The Rent". All You Need Is Love? Not in the 1980s!

At the cinema, the big movies were *Ferris Bueller's Day Off*, *Aliens*, *Top Gun*, *Platoon*, *Blue Velvet*, *Stand By Me* and *Pretty In Pink*.

On TV, 8 September saw the first *Oprah Winfrey Show* broadcast across the US. Other new shows were *L.A. Law*, *Heart Of The City*, *It's Garry Shandling's Show* and *WWF Superstars Of Wrestling*.

In the UK, there were debuts for *Lovejoy*, *Strike It Lucky*, *The Monocled Mutineer*, *Pennies From Heaven* and *Casualty*.

SELECTED TIMELINE 1986–1987

Here is a list of some of the most important dates in the Slippery When Wet *timeline to keep you oriented.*

1986

14 July – Bon Jovi kicked off the *Slippery When Wet* Tour in Vancouver, Canada.
23 July – "You Give Love A Bad Name" was released in the USA.
25 July – The Canadian leg of the tour ended in Ottawa.
9 August – "You Give Love A Bad Name" was released in the UK.
11 August – The Japanese leg of the tour commenced in Nagoya.
18 August – *Slippery When Wet* released in the US.
25 August – The Japanese leg ended in Sapporo.
20 September – *Slippery When Wet* released in the UK.
15 October – *Slippery When Wet* was certified Gold and Platinum in the USA.
25 October – "Livin' On A Prayer" was released in the UK.
31 October – "Livin' On A Prayer" was released in the USA.
7 November – The UK leg of the tour commenced in Bradford.
26 November – The UK leg of the tour ended, also in Bradford; totalling fifteen UK shows.
27 November – Bon Jovi played their first mainland European show in Arnhem, Holland.
8 December – The European leg of the tour ended in Helsinki, Finland.
19 December – The North American leg of the tour commenced in Baltimore, Maryland.

1987

11 April – "Wanted Dead Or Alive" was released in the UK.

10 August – The North American leg of the tour ended in Uniondale, New York.

14 August – *Disorderlies* was released in cinemas in the USA; it features Bon Jovi's "Edge Of A Broken Heart".

14 August – "Never Say Goodbye" was released in the USA.

15 August – "Never Say Goodbye" was released in the UK.

21 August – *Slippery When Wet* was certified 8 x Platinum in the USA.

22 August – Bon Jovi headlined the UK's Monsters Of Rock festival at Castle Donington.

5 September – The Australian leg of the tour commenced in Melbourne.

18 September – The Australian leg of the tour ended in Sydney.

24 September – The final leg of the tour commenced in Tokyo.

7 October – The band played the last of a run of Japanese shows in Shizuoka.

15 October – The band played the first of three shows in Honolulu, Hawaii.

17 October – The band played the very last show of the tour in Honolulu, Hawaii.

PART ONE
SETTING THE SCENE

Did you first own *Slippery When Wet* on vinyl, CD, or even cassette? (*Jan Sandvik Editorial / Alamy*)

1
THE ENDURING APPEAL OF
SLIPPERY WHEN WET

According to Robert Dimery's popular reference book, *Slippery When Wet* is one of the *1001 Albums You Must Hear Before You Die*. Such is the enduring popularity of *Slippery When Wet* that more than 25 years later, it is still spoken about, still played, still selling and still causing debate amongst die hard rock fans. Sure, some of the songs (namely, "Livin' On A Prayer") are overplayed at karaokes, weddings and Bar Mitzvahs, but the band really hit a nerve in the public consciousness with this album.

While Bon Jovi have drifted further and further away from the melodic rock sound of their big-haired youth, *Slippery When Wet* represents a milestone in their career and such is the continuing popularity of the album, the band are often playing songs from it in their current set lists. These days, Bon Jovi are a controversial band within the rock fraternity – the big question being: is Bon Jovi a rock band anymore? It's debatable. But nevertheless, this little book you have in your hands is about *Slippery When Wet* and, dammit, this album is totally rockin'. It has rock printed all over it. Some would argue that *New Jersey* is a better album; edgier and with more grit, but c'mon, *Slippery When Wet* is something special, isn't it? Who's not familiar with "You Give Love A Bad Name" or "Livin' On A Prayer"? Love 'em or loathe 'em, these songs are here to stay. Young or old, most people know these songs and can recite their choruses almost word for word.

It has given the band material success, though JBJ doesn't reckon that is the prime motivator: "You know, I became a recording artist when I was twenty, twenty-one. I made my first million by the time I was twenty-five," he told Ingrid Sischy of New York's *Interview Magazine* in 1998. "The first hundred million came when I was thirty-five. It means shit to me. What matters is not all the commercial success but the heart that went into that: five kids from Jersey doing what they wanted to do. Same thing with what I'm doing now, in both the music and the movies."

In America alone, *Slippery When Wet* has sold over 12 million copies making it the band's biggest selling album (with global sales of a staggering 28 million), which just goes to show that prophets are sometimes honoured in their own land. *Slippery When Wet* is one of the Top 25 biggest-selling albums of all time and was awarded the Diamond Certificate by the Record Industry Association Of America (RIAA). In the States, it has gone Platinum more than a dozen times and it is also Bon Jovi's biggest selling album in the UK; a country that continues to absolutely adore Bon Jovi.

You can always tell the success of an album by the amount of times it has been reissued, and in 2005 a (slightly premature) 20th Anniversary DualDisc edition was released to celebrate the album's longevity. The CD contained the remastered version of the album while the DVD side of the package contained the same album in its original studio mix but also with an upgraded 5.1 Dolby Surround Sound version, and the expanded version of the album contained new parts to the songs thus increasing the album's length.

You can have a picture disc too, though as that was a collector's edition released at the time, you will have to pay over the odds to secure a copy.

The original album remains incredibly popular with fans and, for many, it's when Bon Jovi started to become interesting and entertaining (although for me, Bon Jovi's first two albums are still underrated melodic rock gems and should be given their dues).

So what helped make (and continues to help make) *Slippery When Wet* so popular? That is the question, as Hamlet observed (but not about this album – maybe he would have been more cheerful if it had been around in his time: "Screw revenge, come on Ophelia, let's dance").

Andrew Leahey says in his review of the special edition album for *All Music*: "*Slippery When Wet* wasn't just a breakthrough album for Bon Jovi; it was a breakthrough for hair metal in general, marking the point where the genre officially entered the mainstream. Released in 1986, it presented a streamlined combination of pop, hard rock, and metal that appealed to everyone – especially girls, whom traditional heavy metal often ignored."

The great Tico Torres circa 1985
(*Bob Leafe/Frank White Agency*)

LET IT ROCK

What do rock reviewers think of the album in the twenty-first century now that 25 years has gone by?

"In my opinion," writes Lesley Aeschliman on the popular site Helium, "*Slippery When Wet* is the best album that Bon Jovi recorded. It had a very strong sense of commercial appeal for its time, and many of the songs can still stand strong over twenty years later. Also, most of my favourite Bon Jovi songs of all-time appear on this album. *Slippery When Wet* is an album I still pull out to listen to on a regular basis."

One reviewer writes on *The Ace Black Blog*: "Bon Jovi's massive global success from Nowheresville USA became an inspiration for aspiring rockers everywhere. While it's popular to dismiss Bon Jovi for their relatively simplistic lyrics and overall fist-pumping ethic, *Slippery When Wet* undoubtedly proves that Bon Jovi could write catchy tunes that entertain without ever pretending to demand effort."

"What should not be underestimated is the partnership between drummer Tico Torres and bassist Alec John Such," writes one unknown person on *Geeks Of Doom*. "This is one truly great rhythm section that just will not quit. Torres is rarely flashy and keeps the power and precision throughout the album ticking over. Similarly, Such keeps the tune ticking over, allowing Sambora to wail to his heart's content ... It continues to spark interest in fans old and new and its songs create defining moments at the band's live shows."

Aside from the aforementioned reissue and the euphoria that has always greeted the album; the band reworked some tracks from *Slippery When Wet* for 2003's *This Left Feels Right*, which saw the band – as the title suggests – taking a left turn. There are many acoustic versions of the band's best known songs and those taken from *Slippery When Wet* are "Wanted Dead Or Alive", "Livin' On A Prayer" and "You Give Love A Bad Name" along with a load of unplugged (as we used to say in the 1990s) versions of songs from other albums.

Richie Sambora spoke to *The Daily Record*'s David Wild about the former two songs: "'Wanted' never surprises me. That and 'Livin' On A

Prayer' – those couple of songs you can't do anything to mess up. 'Prayer' is so new and so good. We figured if we're going the other way, why not have a woman sing this with Jon? That way it will be a whole different thing – almost like a conversation. We talked about some people, but then Pat [producer Patrick Leonard] played a demo tape of his [then] wife Olivia D'Abo who's an actress and a singer [and also the daughter of Mike D'Abo of Manfred Mann fame]. I immediately volunteered to play guitar on her record for free. She really had the vulnerability that I heard in my head."

Even though the band have tried desperately hard to move away from their 1980s hair metal image and those catchy commercial pop-rock songs, they represent a period in time both in the band's history and the annals of rock. "I rarely listen to the old records. There's not even a platinum record hanging in my house," JBJ told VH-1 in 2002. "But I heard 'You Give Love A Bad Name' on the radio the other night. I turned it up, too. I was like, 'Wow. It's still on the radio, all these years later.' I saw myself as a younger kid, enjoying that moment in time, and you smile. It still holds up."

Slippery When Wet was, naturally, of its time. In the same way that *Sgt. Pepper* defined the Summer of Love in 1967, or Bowie's *Low* perfectly captured the ennui of the mid-1970s, so *Slippery When Wet* sums up the opulent 1980s. It is a big album produced by men with big hair, who produced big sounds for big venues. Had 1985's *Live Aid* been held two years later, surely Bon Jovi would have been on the bill (they were at *Farm Aid* in the same year), because they were made for the big arenas (and, to their eternal credit, always happy to help people less fortunate than themselves – which, by the end of the 1980s as their earnings skyrocketed, was most people). Bob Geldof joining the band on stage at Wembley Stadium in 1995 (and reprising the role in 2010 at the O2 Arena) is the Papal Blessing from the pontiff of pop.

The album exudes confidence and much of America felt confident too. The Iranian Hostage crisis was five years in the past and America was on the up. Whatever else you may think about Ronald Reagan, he had confidence – boy, did he have confidence. The Star Wars project may have been unworkable, but it was a big dream to dream. The Cold War wasn't over, but it was lukewarm rather than icy and it was becoming increasingly apparent that western values would triumph, with the peoples of Eastern Europe wanting a piece of Uncle Sam's apple pie, not the austerity borsch that had previously been served up to them. The Wall wasn't going to come tumbling down until the end of the decade, but due to Mikhail Gorbachev's willingness to reform, the cracks were starting to appear.

That is not to say that Bon Jovi necessarily subscribed to this viewpoint or that it consciously affected them, but the feel good factor was catching and the late 1980s was party central time. It wasn't until the 1990s that the hangovers started to kick in and we all went unplugged as the party ended and a new movement came to town. It was like the English Civil War, with gallant Hair Metal Cavaliers being supplanted by dowdy Grunge Roundheads.

Slippery When Wet was especially popular with women – not only due to the nature and style of the songs, but because JBJ and Sambora were cute. If you look at the audience at a typical heavy metal gig, it is very male dominated, whereas Bon Jovi have a more even split. That, in turn, makes it more desirable for lads to go to see the band in the hope that the girls will be whipped into a sexual frenzy by Jon and the boys and be ready to settle for second best (that's the theory anyway).

Finally, Ricky Phillips of Styx and formerly The Babys and Bad English told me: "*Slippery When Wet* was a well-crafted and performed album that stylistically hit all the sweet spots of '80s radio dead on the money. It was a visual time when musicians didn't look like they just got off work at Kinko's so Jon's model good looks didn't hurt. But he backed it up with strong vocals and the band was powerful. Looking back it's no wonder they dominated the radio charts, got maximum airplay on MTV and had huge record sales and concert attendance."

2
THE FIRST TWO BON JOVI ALBUMS

Like a pair of unwanted orphans, Bon Jovi's first two albums are rarely mentioned in polite society, with many people, wrongly, considering *Slippery When Wet* to be the first born in the Bon Jovi family. Whisper who dares, but, in actual fact, the first two albums – especially their second one – are pretty hot stuff. They're certainly not earth-shattering, but they ain't half bad. So, let's see what New Jersey's favourite musical sons (with all due respect to Mr B. Springsteen, born in Freehold, N.J.) were up to prior to their elevation to rock's Mount Olympus with *Slippery When Wet*.

"Runaway" was the song that started it all for Mr Jon Bon Jovi or Mr John Francis Bongiovi Jr. as he was born (Bongiovi roughly translates from the Italian as good youth, though Giove is the Italian for Jupiter, which is apt for someone who was to become a rock god). Written by Jon and George Karak, it was originally part of a four track demo that Jon had recorded with a bunch of session musicians working under the moniker of The All Star Review at Power Station Studios in Manhattan as far back as June 1982.

As quoted in *Metal Hammer* (Vol. 5, No. 8), Jon said: "When I was living in New York, 53rd Street ... I'd drive out to Jersey to see my parents, I'd pass by the Greyhound bus station, and all the hookers would hang out there. I'd see these girls who would come out to New York, much the same way they'd come out to Los Angeles, looking for dreams."

The song was picked up by several radio stations, notably the Long Island station WAPP FM 103.5, and it also featured on the compilation *New York Rocks 1983*, released by Doubleday, the parent company of the radio station, with Jon being billed by his real name of John Bongiovi (as an aside, a Long Island band called Twisted Sister contributed a cut to the album called "Shoot 'em Down" - they didn't do so badly in the music business either!). "Runaway" was noticed by one Derek Shulman at PolyGram (a Brit working in New York), who enticed the executive bosses to sign Jon to their label. A deal was done. Jon got himself a band and the wheels for future rock stardom were set in motion.

"I had heard the demo through two routes virtually in the same week," Shulman told me. "The radio station in NYC, WAPP, was featuring local bands and their songs and I heard Jon Bongiovi's 'Runaway' on it; I was very impressed. The next day an attorney, Arthur Mann from Philadelphia, came to my office with a three track demo of 'a kid from N.J.' He played 'Runaway' for me. I was amazed that only the day before I had heard and loved this song. We then set up a meeting with Jon and the band." Spooky coincidence huh?

He continues: "Perhaps the most vivid memory I had, as I started getting to know Jon, was his undeniable star quality and his incredible drive to succeed and be the 'biggest and the best' whether as live musician, as a songwriter or in any other goal that he had set for himself. Even then I knew that nothing would hold him back. He wanted to be 'bigger than Elvis' and he probably is on his way to accomplishing that."

"Runaway" was a powerful song with all the ingredients of a chart hit; very much of its time, which is important for capturing the *zeitgeist*. The staff at PolyGram were very supportive of the song and of JBJ's aim. Shulman had been invited to a showcase at the popular Copacabana club in midtown New York by the band's attorney. JBJ had put together a group of musicians for the showcase (Richie Sambora, David Bryan, Alec John Such and Tico Torres) and played around five or six songs for the record label executives. The band certainly showed they could become huge stars despite the raggedness of their performance. Incidentally, Sambora was not the original guitarist, that honour befell Dave Sabo. However, he was replaced early on. Sabo did all right for himself though, as he went on to form Skid Row. Sambora had previously opened for Joe Cocker when in the band Message and even auditioned for KISS at one stage, so he wasn't exactly a beginner.

However, PolyGram was not the only label interested in putting the New Jersey singer's signature on a contract; Atlantic had sniffed around too before passing. Shulman was adamant that PolyGram should sign JBJ and the band. Jon, his family and the rest of the band were impressed by Shulman's commitment and enthusiasm, which made them feel comfortable with this "limey".

By the way, Derek Shulman wasn't just any old record company executive, he had had a very successful musical career before becoming "a suit" (not that record company executives wore suits anymore, but you know what I mean). He was the lead singer of Simon Dupree And The Big Sound (there was no Simon Dupree, they just thought the name sounded good), a well-respected 1960s pop band whose biggest hit was "Kites". He then went on to form Gentle Giant with his brothers Phil and Ray, plus Kerry Minnear, Gary Green and Martin Smith (the latter was the drummer and was replaced after the second album by Malcolm Mortimore, who in turn was replaced by John "Pugwash" Weathers).

In case the name Gentle Giant doesn't ring any bells (and the band were never as huge as their talents merited), they were British progressive rockers *extraordinaire*. Multi-instrumentalists, they merged many different musical styles – rock, folk, classical, jazz, blues, even madrigals, with non-standard chord progressions, complex key and time changes that left many other hardened prog rock bands scratching their collective heads and wondering how the hell they managed it.

Do give them a listen if you get a chance, if only to marvel at how Derek Shulman, with his prog rock background, managed to de-tune his radar to rockers like Bon Jovi and spot their star quality.

It was obvious from the start that it was JBJ's band, as Shulman attests: "Jon did in fact want to be signed as a solo artist with his band in tow. PolyGram ultimately signed all the players of the band, but initially it was Jon's deal. Rightly so, as it was he who put everything together for the deal to happen ... He absolutely knew he wanted this to be a rock band. He had already put this showcase band together and we both wanted the band to be a band not a solo rocker. He ultimately stuck with the group of musicians who performed at the Copacabana."

With a demo that was destined for cult status, a record deal and a band, JBJ had taken the first tentative steps on the road to becoming a rock star. He had also got a name for his band: Bon Jovi. Lots of names were thrown around but none of them seemed to work. It was Shulman who came to the rescue with the idea of shortening Jon's second name "Bongiovi" to "Bon Jovi" thus taking a leaf out of Van Halen's book (The Bongiovi clan originally came over from Sicily, his dad was a hairdresser – I don't think he did Jon's hair during the *Slippery When Wet* period!). This meant that both Jon Bon Jovi and his band could be marketed more effectively.

Left: Didn't anyone ever tell Jon not to play with fire extinguishers! (*Tony Mottram*)

"I remember saying to him in 1983: 'Someday you'll be President of the United States of America,'" Shulman recalls. "He laughed, but with a glint in his eye. I still stand by that statement." Well, why not? In the 1960s there was LBJ, so why not a JBJ now?

Having acquired a record deal with PolyGram, Messrs Jon Bon Jovi, Richie Sambora, David Bryan, Alec John Such and Tico Torres began work on what was to become their eponymously titled debut album in June 1983. Recording took place at New York City's Power Station Studios with Lance Quinn and Tony Bongiovi (a cousin of JBJ's father). Though much of the songwriting was done by JBJ, Sambora and Bryan, the band did in fact re-record "Runaway", which was co-written by Jon Bon Jovi and George Karak. As mentioned, JBJ had previously recorded with The All Star Review session band, comprising drummer Frankie La Roca, guitarist Tim Pierce, bassist Hugh McDonald and E Street Band pianist Roy Bittan. (The band wrote the other album tracks except for "She Don't Know" which was written solely by the American keyboardist Marc Avsec and "Shot Through The Heart" which was a co-write by Jon Bon Jovi and Jack Ponti.)

The nifty keyboard intro to "Runaway" was penned by Mick Seeley, later of Southside Johnny And The Asbury Dukes. When the single was released in the States in February 1984 it reached Number 39 in the *Billboard* Hot 100, which isn't bad for a first effort. The accompanying video was filmed over a three day period at Silver City Studios in Queens and was made for approximately $60,000. The band were purportedly not happy with their first ever music video, but had no option as it was required by the record company.

Released in the UK on 28 April 1984, *Bon Jovi* peaked at a disappointing Number 71, though in the States it climbed to a slightly healthier Number 43. The band toured hard in those days, and it's because of their strict work ethic and some heavy promotion that the album went on to sell around two million copies worldwide. However, it did appear to some fans and critics that the album was perhaps more of a solo endeavour for JBJ. The cover shows the singer on his own in a street without the rest of the band, although there is a band shot on the back of the album's sleeve. Incidentally, keyboard player David Bryan was billed as David Rushbaum, his full name being David Bryan Rushbaum.

Paul Suter - one of *Kerrang!*'s top writers at the time - hailed the album as a "magnificent debut" in his review for the publication.

However, bassist Alec John Such told *RAW* magazine in 1993: "I never play it! I'm not too fond of either of our first two records, we really didn't get the chance to show what we could do with either of them ... To me, it's a solid four out of ten."

I think he is being harsh and that *Bon Jovi* is an underrated album and should be given more respect by band and fanbase alike. However, it's not without its flaws: the songwriting has a certain naivety and JBJ's voice is somewhat shallow, but these things take time. There are some great melodic rock tracks, namely "Runaway" and "She Don't Know Me", while "Love Lies" is an effective ballad in its own right. Perhaps the best track on the album is the excellent "Breakout" which has some killer synths, a catchy melody and a sing along chorus. At only nine tracks, it's not an overly long album, but it does show that the five members of Bon Jovi had the right chemistry and knew how to make a good tune. What they needed was a more experienced producer for this kind of music, someone able to take them to greater heights and really push their talents. They needed a batch of hit singles and a hit album!

However, Bon Jovi were really coming out of their shell as a live band. Even though for much of 1984's Bon Jovi Tour they were support act for other artists, Bon Jovi were headliners at the Syria Mosque Theater in Pittsburgh and on the Super Rock '84 Tour in Japan. They also made their first appearance at New York's famed Madison Square Garden. They were steadily building up a reputation as an excellent live act and songs like "Breakout", "Get Ready" and "Runaway" were proving to be crowd pleasers.

Derek Shulman says, "To be honest, Jon and myself would confer regularly about how and in what market he should be developed in. We discussed at length whether he might be construed as the new Rex Smith or the new Van Halen. Obviously, Jon and the band ultimately wanted the latter as did I. In so doing to get the 'rock audience' behind him and the band, they started touring incessantly with the biggest and heaviest rock bands of the day. Not just in the USA, but all over the world. I was amazed and loved the band's work ethic. Nothing was too small, too far, too anything for them to go out and win fans. This has been the secret to their longevity."

There is a parallel here with Iron Maiden, who also broke through in the 1980s. The leader of that particular group is, of course, bassist Steve Harris, who is as equally driven as JBJ. In addition to talent, Maiden got to the top by hard graft, attention to detail and long gruelling tours. They say that genius is 99% perspiration and 1% inspiration and these two examples from different sides of the Atlantic prove that. Those who try to take the short cut via reality TV shows might like to ponder this.

When it came to working on their second studio album, *7800° Fahrenheit*, Bon Jovi had severed the familial tie by not working with Tony Bongiovi or Power Station Studios. *7800° Fahrenheit* was recorded during January/February of 1985 at Philadelphia's The Warehouse with producer Lance Quinn. Many of the album's songs were penned by JBJ, Bryan and Sambora, with the exception of "Secret Dreams" which was written by JBJ, Sambora, Torres and Bill Grabowski. The States uses Fahrenheit rather than Celsius and *7800° Fahrenheit* is the temperature at which stone liquefies, so pretty hot! The inference, of course, is that this album is hotter than a Texas chilli.

Released on 11 May 1985 in the UK, *7800° Fahrenheit* made it to Number 28 in the Top 40 and spent twelve weeks in the album charts. In America, it had been released on 27 March and reached Number 37. The album title was hot, but the reviews were lukewarm and sales were tepid, poorer in fact than *Bon Jovi*, with around one million sold worldwide. However, sales were high enough for the band to earn a Gold disc which put them in a

LET IT ROCK

good mood. But was a Gold record enough? "My only rock star friend was Aldo Nova and he had one gold album that hung above his fireplace," JBJ told VH-1 for their *Ultimate Albums* series in 2002. "He had this – in my eyes – mansion on Long Island. I thought that was it. At that time, though, bands had three records to make or break themselves. We knew we were either going to achieve greater success or be relegated to the theater circuit. You were either going to be Southside Johnny or Def Leppard. I wasn't too concerned because I was 24 years old. But there was a great anticipation for the third record at radio and MTV and the rock magazines."

The marketing campaign for the third single, "Silent Night", unimaginatively declared Bon Jovi as "The Best Kept Secret In Rock 'n' Roll" with a picture of JBJ as America's new rock star in the making. Yet again, the album had just JBJ on the front sleeve, although there is a band shot on the back making it seem like a more unified release. Bon Jovi was a band effort; not a solo project for the front man. Not everybody saw it that way, however.

Howard Johnson wrote in *Kerrang!*: "I can only say that this is a pale imitation of the Bon Jovi we have got to know and learnt to love."

Sounds scribe Mary Anne Hobbs penned a review saying, "… the sad new opus barely bubbles at ten degrees, let alone erupting in the dangerous fashion that its moniker would have us believe …"

While the critics were quick to attack the album, the band have rarely spoken about it since its release. They have blamed production and a tight schedule for its lacklustre performance. They rarely play any songs from the album on tour and it seems that *7800° Fahrenheit* has all but been forgotten about. In Osaka, Japan during the One Wild Night Live tour in 2001 they played "Tokyo Road" probably because that particular tour was a celebration of their entire touring career so far and they were in Japan after all.

7800° Fahrenheit showed that at the time Bon Jovi still needed to work on their lyrics, with most of the songs sounding a little naive. However, it is not the bad album many were led to believe and some tracks have stood the test of time. There are some excellent melodies and Sambora delivers some killer riffs.

7800° Fahrenheit is probably one of their heaviest sounding albums to date, with "The Hardest Part Is The Night" and "Tokyo Road" being two standout tracks. "King Of The Mountain" has a progressive edge to it and "In And Out Of Love" is the kind of song that this band excels at. There are some dulcet harmonies and memorable melodies making *7800° Fahrenheit* a pleasing, if underrated, melodic rock album.

However, despite the relative commercial failure of the album, Bon Jovi went out on the road for the first time as headliners after playing in Munich, Germany in May 1985. The world road jaunt hit the Far East for some dates in Tokyo, Nagoya, Osaka and Sapporo. In Europe, they played France, Sweden, Finland, Germany and Holland before they played around the UK hitting such rock friendly spots as Manchester, Birmingham, London, Newcastle and Edinburgh, with Lee Aaron supporting them in the UK.

Back home in the USA, they supported Ratt on tour, which showed that perhaps Bon Jovi were a bigger name outside of their native country. During the tour with Ratt they flew to England for a spot at the famed Monsters Of Rock festival on 17 August 1985.

The band knew how to make a good rock tune, but not the kind of album that could compete with the burgeoning glam rock scene in California which was dominating the *Billboard* charts.

Derek Shulman recalls, "Bon Jovi fitted into the mainstream rock marketplace in virtually the same way as Mötley Crüe and Def Leppard did. Most of these bands appealed to both a male and female audience. This was NOT metal; it was rock with great songs and not just attitude. The hair, clothes, and the advent of MTV helped make this genre enormous. The key thing about Bon Jovi was that he/they did appeal to a female audience without alienating their male audience. On tour, they would rock as hard as the Scorpions, KISS, Van Halen, etc., while still making the females in the crowd want to take him/them home.

LET IT ROCK

Both *Bon Jovi* and *7800° Fahrenheit* can be seen as sowing the seeds of superstardom, but the band were not yet the finished article. This isn't surprising as it takes most bands time to find their feet. If they were to ever make it humungously big they needed to up their game to make the sort of album that would have enough global impact to launch them into the premier league of rock players ... and that's exactly what they did.

Shades store is, sadly, no longer with us, but it was a really intimate place to meet the band.

PART TWO
SLIPPERY WHEN WET

Dot and Liz, two well known faces on the London rock scene of the late 1980s, seen here with Jon at the Shades event. Dot is wearing the striped strides.
(*Tony Mottram*)

3
IN THE STUDIO

Despite having released two albums on a major label, Bon Jovi were not making much money and were paying their crew more than they were paying themselves. Every cent they made was ploughed back into the band. They were also in debt to their record label to the tune of a couple of million dollars. The band were working their collective asses off without receiving their just deserts.

However, after the nine month world tour to promote their second album they were living the dream, and loving every minute of it, even though when they weren't touring they came down to earth with a bump, as they were still living with their folks back home in NJ. They craved a *bona fide* hit record. They had become a fantastic live band but what they needed was an opportunity to have a Number 1 album.

What they needed to do was to recreate in the studio what they were knocking audiences dead with all over the world, as well as up the quality of their songs. They say that fortune favours the brave, and the band took a bold decision in hiring a relatively unknown songwriter, Desmond Child, on the recommendation of KISS front man Paul Stanley, as well as Derek Shulman. Stanley and Child had previously written the disco-themed KISS track "I Was Made For Lovin' You", which features on the 1979 KISS album *Dynasty*, as well as some stuff for Cher. He has since gone on to be one of music's most successful writers. It is probably easier to say which artists he hasn't written for, or with, rather than which ones he has, but just to name check a few: Aerosmith, Katy Perry, Ricky Martin, Meat Loaf and Robbie Williams.

LET IT ROCK

JBJ told VH-1 in 2002 how he and the band got together with Desmond Child: "I liked what Bryan Adams was doing with Tina Turner. So I asked our A&R guy, 'Can't I write a song for a Tina Turner and sing it with her?' He said: 'It's the publisher's job to get those songs out there, and your publisher's obviously not doing that. I know a guy who has lost his record deal and is hustling songs around. If you guys write with him, perhaps something good will come of it.' We thought: 'Why not? We'll see what happens.'" What happened was that Child, Sambora and JBJ wrote over 30 songs.

Many tunes were written and demoed at New Jersey Century Productions in Sayreville, New Jersey, while some were written in the basement of Richie Sambora's parents' house. It was in that basement that they famously wrote their second song together, "You Give Love A Bad Name". His parents both worked full-time, so the house was empty. "I would drive over there in my little Datsun 280Z with some pizza, bang on the door, and wake him up at 1p.m.," JBJ told VH-1 in 2002. "We'd write until six when his folks came home for dinner. It was great because it was just us. We knew who we were. We knew it was going to be a different producer who would capture that live element and we were going to have stories to tell."

Interestingly, they wrote with acoustic guitars; even to this day they don't write with electric all that often. You can understand this if you listen to the gorgeously lush intro to "Wanted Dead Or Alive" that many an aspiring guitarist tries to play.

They worked well together, so much so that their songwriting partnership still continues. "The interchange and exchange of energies and ideas is a lot more invigorating," Richie Sambora explained to *Total Guitar*'s Sian Llewellyn in 2000. "It always takes me a lot longer to write by myself because you're battling with your own wit – it's an inner debate. When you have another person or persons that you write with, it helps. We've always welcomed other people."

They were so concerned about the quality of the songs they'd crafted, that they got their own mini-focus groups together by asking a bunch of kids from New Jersey and neighbouring New York for their opinions on the length of the songs. In New York, they became known as the Pizza Parlor Jury as Sambora explained to VH-1 in 2002:

"When we were making the demos in New Jersey, we'd go across the street to the pizza parlor. They knew we were somebody, but they didn't know really who we were. We asked this arbitrary bunch of kids, 'You want to hear some stuff?' It was like a marketing test with these guys. They came in and said: 'Yeah, we like this one. This one gets through and that one doesn't.'"

The band hired Canadian rock producer Bruce Fairbairn, famous for his work with the Canadian rock band Loverboy, as well as albums with Krokus and Blue Öyster Cult, amongst others. However, Fairbairn was not yet the superstar rock producer he would later become. Fairbairn roped in his protégé Bob Rock as mixer. Fairbairn suggested the band move to Vancouver to record their third album: they had recorded the first album in New York and the second one in Philadelphia, so they had been moving in a slightly westerly direction and Vancouver, on Canada's Pacific seaboard, was as far west as you could get without getting your feet wet. It would also be a new experience for them. Fairbairn wanted to get Bon Jovi out of their comfort zone, and he also felt that by relocating the band to Vancouver he would get full control over them. A new recording environment would ultimately prove to be a key element in the success of their third album.

They worked on what was to become *Slippery When Wet* for two months at Little Mountain Sound Studios in Vancouver during the spring and summer of 1986. They even got involved in some pre-production work, which was new territory for them.

Home in Vancouver was a two bedroom apartment. However, in the best rock 'n' roll tradition they trashed it and JBJ and Sambora were evicted by police because of the noise and complaints from neighbours. There were five young testosterone-fuelled guys staying together at that apartment and things got pretty wild. It was a new condo by the river overlooking Vancouver's World Fair. They finished the last few days in Vancouver by living at the Sheraton Hotel.

The band had heard of Fairbairn because of his work with Loverboy, and admired him from a distance. Fairbairn pushed the band to their absolute limits, working all day and into the night. He knew that if the album was going to work, he had to bring them together as a unit and capture their live energy. Fairbairn believed in the band and he, more than anybody, knew how to draw great performances from Bon Jovi in the studio, as he told *Sound on Sound*'s Richard Buskin in 1997: "I think that reflects my experience over the years, being part of a band. That's how I learned to play, and so that's why I'm really not that interested in working with bands that don't - or can't - perform live. For me that's all part and parcel of giving the consumer a product that is true. I really have a problem with records where the end result doesn't represent either the human performance of the artist or any ability on the part of the artist to actually perform that song. I think that's musical fraud, so I stay well away from it." Well said, sir.

Slippery When Wet was the result of a solid six months of writing, demoing, recording and mixing. The sessions went smoothly, although it was a tense period for the band as Bon Jovi simply had to make a knock-'em-dead rock album if they were to top the relatively modest sales of the first two releases. They had to prove themselves with this release; they really had no other option but to create a classic album.

Richie Sambora would later reflect on the songwriting process to *Music Radar*'s Joe Bosso in 2010: "You can take a song into a studio with a producer and you can put all the bells and whistles all over it, but if you don't have the basic architecture of the song and the foundation of the song properly written ... I mean, Jon and I don't walk into the studio with the band without ten songs that are kind of written."

For the third album, the band were comfortable with each other and believed they had got to know each other musically. *Slippery When Wet*

IN THE STUDIO

was perhaps the first album that cemented the songwriting partnership of JBJ and Sambora, as the guitarist would later tell *Guitar World*: "To be honest with you, we rarely have disagreements. I think we've known each other for so long that we kind of know what the other guy is going to like. Songwriting is a give-and-take process, and it can lead to some good, healthy debates. Sometimes it's necessary to push each other out of the comfort zone a little bit. But I would never try to force Jon to record or perform a song he really didn't like. He's gotta sing it, but more than that, he's gotta feel it. And you can bet your bottom dollar that if he isn't feeling it, the 80,000 people in the stadium sure aren't gonna feel it either. Jon and I have written something like 400 songs together. If I love a tune and he doesn't, I'll save it for one of my records. Simple as that."

They continued to find themselves and grow as a band. They'd become a family by this point and each member of the band brought different influences into the studio. Sambora loved Bad Company and Led Zeppelin; JBJ was into Bruce Springsteen, U2 and the AOR band The Babys, fronted by the English singer John Waite, while Alex John Such enjoyed Judas Priest and AC/DC. Other influences included Southside Johnny, Deep Purple and The Beatles. For their third album, Bon Jovi wanted to somehow merge as many influences together on one album, thus giving them the chance to appeal to a wider audience. Merging the band members' individual tastes together created something unique. The album would be powerful and heavy but not heavy metal.

"Right around *Slippery When Wet* is when I think I hit stride," Sambora told *Guitar.com*'s Jeff Perlah. "At that point, my style as a guitar player was a bit more flamboyant. Those were the days when Eddie Van Halen was doing his tricks, and guys like Satriani and Vai were also popular. But at the same time, I wanted to play the right things for the songs, being a big Beatles fan and a guy who like Aerosmith, Led Zeppelin, Eric Clapton, and Muddy Waters. At that point, I also infused the acoustic guitar back into pop music. It was something I mastered playing in those bars early on, but which I didn't have a chance to play on our first two records. "

LET IT ROCK

When it came to choosing and arranging the final tracklisting for *Slippery When Wet*, JBJ was reluctant to add "Livin' On A Prayer", thinking it was not a hit single. Just how wrong was he? Sambora was adamant it was a Number 1 song. It was one song they did not write in Sambora's parents' house, but rather at Desmond Child's apartment in New York. Sambora was late making the session because he had been working with a friend of his the night before. The beginning of the song came out of the session he had with his friend.

They re-recorded the original demo, giving Sambora the chance to add a musical device called a talk box, which gives the song its famous distinctiveness (the original demo of "Livin' On A Prayer" can be found as a hidden track on the box-set *100,000,000 Bon Jovi Fans Can't Be Wrong*).

The band were initially against the idea of using a talk box until they heard it. They also added different drum fills and a new bass line. Sambora loved the way the talk box worked on Peter Frampton and Joe Walsh recordings, but when he told Fairbairn he wanted to use it on "Livin' On A Prayer" the producer thought he was nuts. However, Sambora got his way and it worked really well. It became iconic. Talk box rarely works and many musicians shy away from it but it ended up making Bon Jovi's career in some ways. "Livin' On A Prayer" would become the band's trademark song.

The talk box is a weird implement. There is an effects pedal on the floor, but a plastic tube comes off it which goes all the way to the musician's mouth. By changing the shape of the mouth, the musician modifies the sound that the instrument (typically, a guitar) makes. Sambora liked the sound so much, he has used the talk box on other tracks, such as "It's My Life" from *Crush*. This song namechecks Tommy and Gina from "Livin' On A Prayer", so he may have felt it appropriate to use the talk box for old times' sake.

Sambora told *Total Guitar*'s Sian Llewellyn about the decision to revive the couple in 2000: "I have to say that the Tommy and Gina reference was my idea. Jon wasn't sure if he liked it and I said that the new people coming onto this record aren't gonna know and our old fans are gonna go: 'Thank you.' Our old fans are gonna go: 'You know what? They remember.' And we do. Those characters are ten years evolved now, as

IN THE STUDIO

are we." They also namecheck Frank Sinatra, of course, as the song is about people who do it their own way and don't give up. Did Tommy and Gina make it? We are told in the lyrics they never back down, so hopefully they got their slice of the American Dream. Who knows, in another ten years, maybe Bon Jovi will sing about them being grandparents!

With a majority of the songs on the album, JBJ and his cohorts always thought of the crowd and how each song would move the crowd, and if – because of those songs – they'd steal the headliner's thunder, before they themselves became headliners. They wanted a mixture of rock songs and ballads like "Never Say Goodbye".

For their third album, the band wanted to tell a story with each song rather than recreate "Runaway". They wanted to write about people they knew in NJ and people they grew up with and went to high school with; guys who joined the service or worked in factories, just regular blue-collar guys. If JBJ hadn't learned to play the guitar and joined a band, he would have been one of those guys.

JBJ is very proud of some of those killer numbers on the album, as he told London's *Time Out* in 2010: "I'll probably be most remembered for songs like 'Wanted Dead Or Alive' and 'Living On A Prayer' [*sic*] but you also want [it to be] every song you write. With every latest one, you think: That's it, I've outdone it. What are they going to write in my obituary? 'Wanted Dead Or Alive' and 'Living On A Prayer' [*sic*]. Hey, it's better to have had one. Shit, I've been lucky enough to have had six."

With "Wanted Dead Or Alive", JBJ and Sambora drew some inspiration from legendary Led Zeppelin guitarist Jimmy Page. The pair believed radio lacked acoustic guitars and, after coming up with ideas in the studio, they thought an acoustic sound to the track would work brilliantly. JBJ was also a fan of Bob Dylan and Johnny Cash so in a way the song was a tribute to the two musicians. It was during the Fahrenheit Tour that JBJ got to thinking

LET IT ROCK

about a song like Bob Seger's "Turn The Page" (which was later covered by thrash metallers Metallica in 1998), when he was looking out of the window of the tour bus, unable to sleep, wondering where he was. They were rock stars living the dream; it was an interesting and exciting experience moving from city to city, sleeping and showering on the tour bus. He told Sambora about the idea and the guitarist came up with a riff and within just a few hours they banged out the song. It represented a place in time for the band.

Total Guitar's Chris Bird would later note Sambora's effectiveness on the album: "His riffs are as integral to the band's songs as Jon's lead vocals. His solos always transform the direction of a song and take it somewhere new. Richie's ear for melody means he solos with the bare minimum of widdly-ness, but still with the odd searing lick thrown in for good measure. Examples? 'Livin' On A Prayer', 'You Give Love A Bad Name'."

The band also decided not to include "Edge Of A Broken Heart" which later ended up being used on the soundtrack to the film *Disorderlies*. In total, *Slippery When Wet* includes three songs which were co-written with Desmond Child: "You Give Love A Bad Name", "Livin' On A Prayer" and "Without Love".

It should be mentioned that whilst Child had a hand in writing some of the band's key songs, he didn't write on everything and JBJ was at pains to stress in an interview with Sylvie Simmons for *Request* magazine in 1996 that: "Some people believe that Desmond is responsible for breaking Bon Jovi, but what they forget is that when we worked with him he wasn't the established songwriter that he is now. We helped him as much as he helped us." He has a point, as it was a mutually beneficial relationship, as the best partnerships have to be, and JBJ is no slouch as a songwriter himself, hence his induction into the Songwriters Hall Of Fame in 2009.

In terms of sales, manager Doc McGhee was ecstatic. He told Billboard in September 1986: "We couldn't be happier with the way the record has taken off." He added: "It's incredible how quickly the album went gold and it shouldn't be too long before platinum." He wasn't wrong, he just under-estimated!

Even though it was a tiring album to make and the band worked long hours, they still had a blast, as Sambora would reflect to *The Daily*

Right: A party at Break For The Border restaurant to celebrate *Slippery When Wet* going gold. Manager Doc McGhee is at the front with a moustache. (*Tony Mottram*)

IN THE STUDIO

Record's David Wild in 2003: "*Slippery* was our breaking point, and we knew it. When we were making that record we were having a blast. It was a fun record to make – an easy record to make."

Looking back on the making and eventual success of the album, Bob Rock told Mitch Lafon at *Brave Words & Bloody Knuckles*: "They were fantastic. I just love them. Right from *Slippery*, they were these guys from New Jersey that came in and shook up Vancouver, Bruce Fairbairn and my life. We were just hoping it would go Gold. We were like 'God, if it goes Gold we'll at least get to do another album' and, of course, it did what it did and *New Jersey* did what it did. They're the hardest working guys. They're the nicest guys and in terms of commitment to his career and his band, Jon is second to no one. I can't comment on what they do today except it seems that he always seems to redefine what it is so that he can keep doing it. It's amazing what he does."

Desmond Child, Bruce Fairbairn, Bob Rock and Bon Jovi were all on the brink of success and *Slippery When Wet* would bring them all fame and fortune.

"After *Slippery When Wet* I thought I was a fake, that it was a fluke," JBJ told *Glamour Magazine* in 2003. "I didn't believe I could do it again. I thought, 'You know, I don't think I can do it again so I have to prove I can.' My insecurity almost killed me and the band."

4
A SONG BY SONG REVIEW

Musicians on all tracks:
Jon Bon Jovi – lead vocals, guitar, Richie Sambora – guitar, backing vocals, Alec John Such – bass, backing vocals, Tico Torres – drums, David Bryan – keyboards, backing vocals

1. LET IT ROCK (*JBJ/Sambora*) 5:27
Well, "Let It Rock" is a great way to start the album: in many ways this five minute track is the personification of commercial American arena rock. David Bryan gives it some gravitas with the opening organ playing what is known as "Pink Flamingos" in the key of D. This gives the listener the feeling that this is going to be something special, something grandiose. It could almost be the start of a progressive rock album, but, of course, it's not. It might not be as regularly played as some of its *Slippery When Wet* siblings, but it's one of the album's standout tracks. Smooth melody, well-crafted guitars, dulcet vocals and some indelible lyrics, "Let It Rock" is the perfect introduction to '80s Bon Jovi. There's definitely a hint of Def Leppard here circa *Pyromania*, but it makes the track all the stronger for it. This opening is a statement of intent – this baby is gonna rock your socks off.

2. YOU GIVE LOVE A BAD NAME (*JBJ/Sambora/Child*) (3:44)
"You Give Love A Bad Name" was originally written for the Canadian rock band Loverboy, but, call it fate or just plain old good luck, Bon Jovi kept it for themselves. It features the same line as the title of one of their tracks off their first album, of course, namely "Shot Through The Heart".

It's often been compared to another Desmond Child penned song called "If You Were A Woman And I Was A Man" recorded by Welsh singer Bonnie Tyler, and indeed the melodies do have some similarities. For those who like a bit of gossip, some say the song is about Jon Bon Jovi's brief relationship with the actress Diane Lane, but who really knows? What we do know, is it is one helluva good rock song; a catchy melody, sing-along chorus and some memorable guitars. Such is its appeal that "You Give Love A Bad Name" has been a permanent fixture in Bon Jovi's set lists. The only full colour music video from *Slippery When Wet*, "You Give Love A Bad Name" was filmed at the Olympic Auditorium in Los Angeles, California.

It was the first single release from *Slippery When Wet*. It was issued in the UK on 9 August 1986 and only peaked at Number 14 although it did spend ten weeks in the singles chart. On the other hand, it hit top spot in the *Billboard* Hot 100 on 29 November. It was Bon Jovi's first Number 1 single and went on to sell well over one million copies – kerching!

3. LIVIN' ON A PRAYER (*JBJ/Sambora/Child*) (4:09)
If Bon Jovi have a theme tune, it would have to be this, surely their best loved number. Tommy and Gina are scratching a living in Ronald Reagan's America, where Tommy is on strike. They may be victims of the Reaganomics mentioned in Simply Red's version of The Valentine Brothers' song "Money's Too Tight (To Mention)" the previous year. JBJ is a Democrat and campaigned on behalf of John Kerry in 2004, so this analysis isn't too far-fetched.

Some on the political right have tried to claim it for their own claiming that Tommy was a strike breaker, which would make him a hero to them (though a scab or blackleg to those on the left). However, in a fascinating interview in *The Guardian* (5/11/2009), where journalist Caroline Sullivan brokered an unlikely interview between JBJ and Creation Records boss Alan McGee (who is not a Bon Jovi admirer), Jon tells us: He just lost his job – it wasn't that he crossed the [picket] line. The industry left the town and he didn't get the job back."

LET IT ROCK

The promotional video was filmed at the Mayo Civic Center in Rochester, Minnesota. "Livin' On A Prayer" is probably Bon Jovi's most famous song and has been played at weddings, parties, student nights and various other social occasions ever since. It's a fun song with a nifty melody, a toe-tapping arms-in-the-air chorus and, as mentioned earlier, the good old talk box, which Sambora also uses during the live versions of "Livin' On A Prayer". It is another of the album's songs that has been played repeatedly at Bon Jovi concerts since 1986. The video won them the Best Performance award at the MTV Music Awards in California in 1987.

Part of the song's appeal is that it starts with a minor chord (E minor) which gives the tension that is resolved by the killer chorus which starts with a C chord. Like many great rock songs, it doesn't try to over elaborate with loads of chords – it keeps it simple.

It was the second single release from *Slippery When Wet* and was written by Jon, Sambora and Desmond Child. It was released in the UK on 25 October 1986 and peaked at Number 4, spending fifteen weeks in the charts. In the States, it was the second single from the album to hit Number 1 in the *Billboard* Hot 100.

In one of those quirks of fate, the song re-entered the *Billboard* chart many years later getting to number 25 in November 2013. A fan of the Boston Celtics, Jeremy Fry, was caught on camera dancing around wildly to the song as it was played at one of the baseball team's games. He is really getting into it and several other fans join in and the whole thing went viral.

4. SOCIAL DISEASE (*JBJ/Sambora*) (4:18)

Pop rock, soft rock, melodic rock; whatever you want to call it, "Social Disease" is similar to "Let It Rock" in that it's an immaculately crafted rock song, perhaps too polished, but it is a fine representation of the time.

Talking about of its time, the 1980s was the decade when AIDS really first hit the public consciousness. The song appears to be talking about love itself as the disease rather than an STD, though love is described as an infection. It is possible that sub-consciously sexually transmitted diseases helped inspire the lyric, who knows? What we do know, is that big-hearted Jon has worked on behalf of the Elizabeth Glaser Pediatric AIDS Foundation, a charity dedicated to raising awareness of HIV in children.

To quote a cliché, this is the kind of song that will really rock your world. The production is top-notch, Sambora delivers some strong guitars and the melody is consistently catchy. The horns add to the overall feel, giving it a slightly funky edge.

It's glossy American soft rock and easily accessible to the masses. Nothing wrong with that.

5. WANTED DEAD OR ALIVE (*JBJ/Sambora*) (5:08)
Written in homage to the American Old West and inspired by Bob Seger's "Turn The Page", the fifth track on *Slippery When Wet* is another one of the album's most iconic tracks. The story goes that "Wanted Dead Or Alive" was written sometime on tour in 1985, as previously mentioned. The image of the cowboy is very strong in the American consciousness, of course, even amongst east coasters like Bon Jovi. Cowboys used to ride the range, maybe taking cattle along the Chisholm Trail, a peripatetic existence that requires a certain mindset. The modern cowboy is the touring rock star riding in the bus from town to town – as much a drifter as the cowboy.

It's another perfectly crafted song with a lovely melody and it really captures the sound of the Old West, albeit with glossy effects. The descending guitar intro really sets the scene as it sounds reminiscent of a Spanish guitar, which isn't surprising as Sambora is a big fan of this style of playing. One thing that gives the song its edge is that the intro is in D minor whereas the verse starts in D major. You don't need to be a musician to appreciate this, it hits you at ear level as something different and therefore melodically interesting.

Along with the duo of "You Give Love A Bad Name" and "Livin' On A Prayer", "Wanted Dead Or Alive" has been regularly performed on tour. It is a nice change of pace from some of the rockier numbers. The music video was filmed at various arenas around the USA and features black and white footage from Bon Jovi's gruelling *Slippery When Wet* World Tour of 1986-87. The song was re-recorded for the 2003 album *This Left Feels Right*.

It was released in the UK on 11 April 1987 and it reached Number 13, spending seven weeks in the charts. It peaked at Number 7 in the *Billboard* Hot 100. It was the third Top 10 single in the States for the band from just one album, making them the only American rock band at that point to achieve such a record. Recently, the song has been used as the lead theme for the US reality TV show *Dog The Bounty Hunter*.

On tour this song got extended into a showcase for Sambora's tasty playing. He often used an Ovation double neck, and even a triple neck, which were custom built for him. These had 6 and 12 string necks, which allowed him to switch depending on whether he wanted the fuller sound of the 12 string or not. Double and triple necked guitars also resonate really nicely too. Trouble is, they are heavy and unwieldy to play – not that it seemed to bother Richie. Incidentally, he isn't wedded to one make of guitar. He also used a rare Rod Schoepfer Custom Les Paul on much of *Slippery When Wet*. Like many professional players, he is a bit of a guitar junkie with a reputed collection of over 120 guitars.

Here endeth the first side.

6. RAISE YOUR HANDS (*JBJ/Sambora*) (4:16)
Kicking off side two is "Raise Your Hands", another cheery hard rocker with a catchy singalong chorus, a killer melody. This is the kind of arena rock song that isn't made anymore. It's very much a song of its time; when you listen to it you can see in your mind's eye thousands of fans in a packed arena, arms stretched in the air with lighters (these days, mobile phones) in their hands singing along to the chorus. It's a solid rock song that's not as heavy as songs by bands like Quiet Riot and Ratt, but more like Def Leppard, with a killer guitar solo. It's glossy, it's commercial and has more polish than your gran's best sideboard, but that doesn't stop it from being a hugely enjoyable song. In sum: it is an FM classic!

7. WITHOUT LOVE (*JBJ/Sambora/Child*) (3:30)

To some rock fans, "Without Love" may be considered a disposable song with lightweight lyrics and a throwaway melody, but to others it is a cherished rock ballad with the universal message that we all need to be loved. The chorus is as catchy as hell and great to sing along to and a slower number at this point in the album fits. The exaggerated guitars work really well with this song and JBJ carries the notes perfectly. Bon Jovi have made some very famous and often iconic rock ballads and "Without Love" is an example of classic 1980s rock, or is it rawk? What the heck, we all need love!

8. I'D DIE FOR YOU (*JBJ/Sambora*) (4:30)

A slightly more up-tempo ballad than other songs on the album, "I'd Die For You" is typical Bon Jovi with respect to the lyrics and the melody – even the title itself is pure Bon Jovi. It's not the strongest track on the album and on its own it's nothing to rave about, but within the context of the entire album it works really well and is very anthemic and epic, which means it is well suited to the live environment. It starts off with the piano before Sambora kicks in with the guitar as if to say to Bryan, "It's my turn now".

The sentiments are spot on for teenage (or even older) love. In that first flush we like to think we would do anything for the object of our affections up to and including dying for them (the question is, what happens when that feeling wears off!).

9. NEVER SAY GOODBYE (*JBJ/Sambora*) (4:48)

A love ballad, 'Never Say Goodbye' is a mid-tempo song with long drawn-out vocals typical of 1980s power ballads. This is the chance for the listener to take a breather during a slower song. Some people think it is a disposable number, but most albums have reflective moments: think of Black Sabbath's *Volume 4* – a really heavy album if ever there was one – which featured the ballad "Changes" (even if you don't know much about Sabbath, you'll know this tune, which was also a hit single for Kelly and Ozzy Osbourne in 2003). My point is, if the godfathers of metal can slow things down then anyone can!

LET IT ROCK

The premise of "Never Say Goodbye" concerns a couple who try to stay together amidst the difficulties of youth. It's occasionally played live, and in the early days was an excuse for JBJ to "fly" across an arena (with wires of course, not even he can fly unaided!). As Richie Sambora told Simon Witter of the *NME* in December 1988 "Jon thought up the wire thing so that he could go to the kids at the back of the hall and make them feel special,"

Lyrically, it is a very American song (not surprising, I hear you say, as the band are from the US), with its theme of lost youth, making out in a car (in fact, taking the girl's virginity), beer, the radio and other staples of the American teen experience. Jim Steinman is another songwriter who vividly paints a picture of American teen life, perhaps most famously on 1977's *Bat Out Of Hell* track "Paradise By The Dashboard Light", where Meat Loaf trades promises of lifelong fidelity in exchange for car sex with female singer Ellen Foley and then lives to regret it.

In the UK, it is more likely to be a snog and a grope at the bus stop whilst waiting for the last bus home, but the sentiments are still the same.

The fourth and final single from *Slippery When Wet*, it was released in the UK on 15 August 1987. It reached Number 21 in the Top 40 and spent five weeks in the charts. It fared less well in America, hitting Number 28 in the *Billboard* Hot 100. The European release came with a live version of "Shot Through The Heart" and the American version came with the previously unreleased "Edge Of A Broken Heart".

Sambora's simple intro (parts of which are repeated throughout the song) is only fifteen notes long, but he manages to extract maximum feeling from those notes and this is a seriously tasteful riff that shows that it isn't how many notes you play, it's about how much feeling you put into what you are playing.

10. WILD IN THE STREETS (*JBJ*) (3:54)

Do you remember your first time? First time of listening to *Slippery When Wet* that is. What did you think I was referring to! You'd maybe bought it on the strength of the singles, or you'd read a glowing review. As you glide into this final track, you realize it's the perfect way to finish the album; from the opening organ of "Let It Rock" to the end of "Wild In The Streets", you're taken on a ride, and what an exhilarating journey it is. I would argue that this album is very well constructed and paced and you want to leave the listener on an up, hence this rocker to end proceedings. Bon Jovi wore their influences on their sleeves and with this song they've made a nod towards Def Leppard with a bit of Springsteen thrown in and it is one of the most poetic lyrics on the album, really painting a picture of someone's experiences in their own town. Again, the themes are staples of the American teen experience: cars, making out on the backseat (which the band seemed to do more than their fair share of, lucky so and so's), a dad that doesn't like the boy and even the reference to the boy's brigade, give this song a heart and a pinpoint in time.

This certainly isn't *Happy Days* with the Fonz (which never really existed outside of TV), is harder than the world of "Jack And Diane" that John Mellencamp described in 1982 (though some of the motivations are the same, making out on the well-worn car backseat; the suspension on American cars must be really robust), but it isn't the world of industrial unrest that Tommy and Gina are experiencing in "Livin' On A Prayer". Rather, it is a warts and all sketch of life in a small town - good and bad. However, no matter what happens, your hometown is always where your heart is.

JBJ neatly summed up the track to Simon Witter of the *NME* in December 1988, saying the song: "captures an emotion of youth, it's about a feeling that is probably true for every generation. My grandfather was probably getting laid in the back of a horse and carriage."

This song closes what is a glorious ten track melodic rock gem.

Publicity shot of the band from the time of *Slippery When Wet*.(Patrick Harbron)

SUMMARY

The fact is that *Slippery When Wet* is one of the greatest rock albums of its kind of all time. Sure, it's not perfect but it's not far off the mark. "Never Say Goodbye" might be too soppy for some but a heady mix of hard rock songs and ballads is what Bon Jovi have always been about. *Slippery When Wet* is heavy without being heavy metal. The production is fantastic, giving both Sambora and JBJ space to breathe. The melodies are wonderful and the lyrics were certainly the best written of the first three albums. It was a coup for the band to hook up with both Desmond Child and Bruce Fairbairn.

JBJ has more confidence and hits the notes with more stride (check out the impassioned pleas on "Never Say Goodbye") and verve, while there are moments of absolute brilliance courtesy of Sambora, such as the talk box during "Livin' On A Prayer". It's not pop metal, it's melodic hard rock and it remains one of the greatest rock albums of all time for a reason. It represents a time in their career that they will never recapture (not that they are keen to; that much is obvious from their later albums). Rather than mourning the fact that Bon Jovi may never make an album that rocks this strong again, rejoice in the fact that they did.

5
THE COVER SLEEVE

Like many famous rock albums Bon Jovi's most successful album to date has a bit of a back story to it.

One idea was to name the album *Guns 'N Roses* as a tribute to the growing albeit notorious glam rock scene over on the West Coast, (more specifically, Los Angeles) but that idea was scrapped ... and for the better!

Another idea that they toyed with was to call it *Wanted Dead Or Alive*. Photographer Mark Weiss recalls, "The first cover was actually them dressed up like Clint Eastwood; they grew some scruff like out of *The Good, The Bad And The Ugly*. I made a WANTED poster and put them in an abandoned barn [with] 'a hideaway' vibe ... On the way up to the 'hideaway location' we saw this kid. We had this little kid have a cigarette come out of his mouth, dressed up like a cowboy."

However, manager Doc McGhee was apparently not so taken by the idea and, to be fair to him, it does sound like a take on the Eagles' *Desperado* from 1973.

The band had gone up to a remote place in Vancouver called the Whistler and they shot some pictures in the Western garb there, but they were unhappy with what was being produced. It wasn't the best photo session for them. As they were driving back to Vancouver to visit their favourite strip club, No.5, Doc McGhee saw the words "*Slippery When Wet*" on a street sign and said they should do something with it. However, the band were undecided.

"*Slippery When Wet*" was also the title of a Commodores single in 1975, but there is little reason to suppose that the band were influenced by this song when it came to naming their album.

LET IT ROCK

Vancouver was blessed (if that's the right word) with a goodly number of strip joints and they played a part in the making of the album's artwork. Sambora confessed to VH-1 in 2002: "The strip clubs in Vancouver were something that we had never seen before, being from New Jersey. The first day we walked into this strip club, this woman descended from the ceiling down a pole and proceeded to take all her clothes off. When she got in a shower and soaped herself up, we just about lost our tongues. We just sat there and said: 'We will be here everyday.' That energized us through the whole project. Our testosterone was at a very high level back then."

Inspired by the many strip joints in Vancouver's red light district, the band thought of the aforementioned No. 5 club where the dancers would strip off and take showers in front of the paying customers. "We lived in those [strip] joints!" Jon told *Kerrang!* in 1994.

Though various ideas were thrown around, and tried and tested in Vancouver and New Jersey, the first photo used for the album's sleeve was hated by Jon Bon Jovi: it was a photograph of a woman with 34DD sized breasts in a wet yellow T-shirt with *Slippery When Wet* written across her chest as a sort of cheesy homage to the Vancouver strip clubs. The sleeve also has a dreadful pink border around the cover. However, it was too late for a full recall on the album as several hundred thousand copies had already been shipped to Japan. But the rest were destroyed. Always the one with the sense of humour in the band, Richie Sambora told *Kerrang!* in July, 1993: "I'm not ashamed of the original *Slippery When Wet* cover – it's just some chick with big tits!"

There's another story about that version of the album sleeve: the American label Mercury were not entirely convinced by this cover and had the band come up with something less controversial, fearing record stores would not stock an album with such a cover. This was the time of Tipper Gore's PMRC (Parents Music Resource Center), a pressure group that objected to overtly sexual album covers and bad language in rock, metal and rap and wished to censor them. Mercury Records certainly didn't want the PMRC on their case potentially damaging record sales.

THE COVER SLEEVE

The original cover featured in the 2009 *Guitar World* poll Top 20 Most Shocking Banned Album Covers alongside Alice Cooper's *Love It To Death* (this featured Alice doing the schoolboy trick of sticking his thumb through his flies on the original design), The Beatles' *Yesterday And Today* (showing the Fab Four dressed in white coats with hunks of meat and dismembered babies, which was too rich for 1966), Black Crowes' *Amorica* (a close up of a woman's crotch, where she is wearing an itsy bitsy teeny weeny Stars & Stripes bikini with some pubes sticking out. Try waxing dear), Blind Faith's 1969 self-titled record (a topless young girl holding a suspiciously phallic looking airplane), and David Bowie's *Diamond Dogs* from 1974, which showed a canine human hybrid Bowie complete with a dog's wedding tackle.

With little time left, the band had to come up with a new photograph for the album. Photographer Mark Weiss tells his version of events: "Then some rocket scientist at the record company came up with a girl holding a bar of soap in the shower – we spent like $2000 on a bar of soap that said '*Slippery When Wet*'; we hired some hand models for a couple of thousand dollars to hold the bar of soap suggestively ... but that didn't work. We thought it was not cool; after seeing the photos we both agreed. And Jon called me up and said: 'I gotta come over to the studio.'

I said: 'Well, you gotta come up with an idea. What is it?'

'Just get your camera ready ... We'll come up with something. We've got like a day to do it.'

And then he comes up [to the studio] and he said: 'Get a garbage bag!'

I sprayed some water on it and he wrote '*Slippery When Wet*'. Jon was like – don't even show me, that's it!"

So his idea was entirely random?

Weiss: "I don't know how he thought of it. It was raining that day. He just said: 'You know what; I don't want my face on the cover. I don't want the band. I want the music to sell itself.' On the back of the album's sleeve was the picture of the band waving goodbye in a big arena that I shot [for] a video; that was their whole thing. They did all these videos for that album; they weren't playing arenas yet. They were opening up for .38 Special and

LET IT ROCK

different bands, they were just openers. The videos had them with all the lights and pyro; before that KISS was the only one really using pyro. All the hair bands did the same over the years in videos and then in concert."

Weiss shot JBJ's idea there and then and that was it – classic rock history had been made. Sometimes the most basic covers are the most effective. Sambora, however, played up the whole thing as though they were making

UK edition of the *Slippery When Wet* picture disc, US flag and backstage pass. These are prized possessions of top rock photographer Tony Mottram. (*Tony Mottram*)

THE COVER SLEEVE

some kind of artistic stance; that just because JBJ was a good looking kid didn't mean he – or the band – could not write a good song. In time they would get frustrated with the way they were being marketed.

Sambora told *JoyZine*'s Anne Raso: "No pictures on the album cover. We'll give them nothing; we'll just let the music speak for itself.' That's what proved it for us. We had to put ourselves out on the line at that point. It would've been easy for us to put out an album cover with Jon's picture on the front – or the whole band, for that matter."

Slippery When Wet has become one of the most recognized album sleeves in rock history, well, not just rock but popular music history as a whole. It was a simplistic concept but sometimes the most basic ideas prove to be the most enduring. Bon Jovi have never been a band known for great album sleeves, but with *Slippery When Wet*'s basic yet eye-catching photo, they really hit the spot. Period.

6
THE REVIEWS & COMMERCIAL RECEPTION

To say *Slippery When Wet* was a hit is an understatement.

"That kind of success ... that was our third album, the third single on a milestone album called *Slippery When Wet*, where fame was thrust upon us in such a manner that it was hard to grasp and, for me, hard to really enjoy, because it was too much," JBJ told Allison Stewart of *CDNow* in 2001. "Not personally so much as physically, mentally, head-wise, it was the exhaustion of running, of doing the work that went with it. I came to terms with all that stuff and realized how to enjoy it, how to tame the beast, and from then on ... it was a very strange time. We went from being a nice bar band or a scary opening act to have on before you to being this phenomenon, and it was a lot."

Bon Jovi have rarely been praised by the critics. In fact as the years have passed, their music has changed and as their success has reached stratospheric heights, critics have liked them less and less, but that's often the case with successful bands – the old "build 'em up to knock 'em down" routine. Fans and critics of melodic rock, including me, certainly have a fair amount of praise to heap on Bon Jovi's first four albums.

Richie Sambora spoke to *Music Radar*'s Joe Bosso about the ingredients of a good rock album, *Slippery When Wet* itself and its subsequent impact on the band's future fortunes: "Good songs, man. I think it's about the songwriting, I really do – that's a big end of it. There's a couple of things

THE REVIEWS & COMMERCIAL RECEPTION

though: When we were a young band, before even Slippery came out, we looked at each other and we said: 'We are going to tour every place we can.' We didn't have any place to go ... Nobody had any houses, we were broke and we just toured everywhere. Basically, what we did was, we prepared the garden for the flowers to grow. We didn't have any hits till *Slippery*, and then when *Slippery* came out, it was huge everywhere."

Slippery When Wet appeared to go global overnight. It was a monstrous success and – while Def Leppard had taken a famously long time to follow up 1983s Pyromania with Hysteria in 1987 – Bon Jovi came along in '86 and stole their thunder. Though *Slippery When Wet* was released in the USA in August 1986, *Billboard* named it the biggest selling album of 1987, which shows its longevity. "We were playing a Holiday Inn in Sioux Falls, South Dakota, opening for the .38 Special, when our manager flew in to tell his boys, 'You're No.1,'" JBJ told Daily Record's Billy Sloan.

JBJ continued: "We lost our [fuckin'] minds with excitement. The .38 Special said: 'How do you feel about a co-headline tour?' We said: 'Sorry, we're outta here' and scammed promoters to pay for a private jet to get us from gig to gig. It was like a cartoon where our tour bus was traveling to the next town as we flew overhead. We said: 'Take your tour bus and shove it.' I've never got back on another one again until 25 years later."

There is a saying in the music business that the third album is the "difficult" one. Presumably, nobody ever told Bon Jovi that, as *Slippery When Wet* turned the band into superstars. Certainly, the success of the album was not only due in part to its stellar quality but also to Bon Jovi's rigorous touring schedule and a clutch of hit singles. MTV did a lot to help sales of *Slippery When Wet*: with the band's good looks, big hair and rock star attire, their music videos were constantly on MTV's rotation schedules.

It is important to emphasize the role of MTV in the success of Bon Jovi and many other 1980s acts too. By the end of the decade about half of US homes had access to it and it was great exposure, of course. If you were TV friendly, as Michael Jackson was (and your production budget was big), you could really enhance your profile. Even if you weren't classically good looking, or a great mover, you could still use MTV to best advantage; you just had to think laterally. ZZ Top are a prime example of this. Rather than putting themselves at the front of their videos, they used the combination of pretty girls and big cars to build their "brand", whilst the band was often playing in the background – almost like observers of the action, not a part of it, whereas, of course, Michael Jackson was firmly centre stage in, for example, the *Thriller* video.

On the whole though, on MTV as in life generally, it does no harm to be good looking and the camera loved JBJ and the boys. However, JBJ doesn't love the camera, as he told Glenn O'Brien of *SPIN* magazine in 1987: "I hate videos. If you wanted to torture me you'd tie me down and force me to watch our first five videos."

However, MTV is just one element of the mix. For a rock band, as both ZZ Top and Bon Jovi are testimony to, there is no substitute for touring. Rock fans demand to see their heroes live and any band that ignores that does so at their peril. The longevity of Bon Jovi, ZZ Top or good old Iron Maiden is partly due to their being prepared to hit the road Jack for long periods.

JBJ found himself on the cover of some of the world's most popular magazines and, all of a sudden, he was an international celebrity, but not necessarily because of his music, as he told Ingrid Sischy of New York's *Interview Magazine* in 1998: "Ten or eleven years ago, when *Slippery* hit, I was very excited about being on the cover of *Rolling Stone*. Then their reporter turned up, and all she could talk about was, 'You're so cute. And your hair!' I thought to myself: 'If you want to [fuck] me, let's just get on with it.' I was very angry about all of that. But what could I do? Scar my face? Knock my teeth out? After a while, I learned if they're going to say all I am is a pretty face, then they're not taking the time to look at the facts, which speak for themselves."

That is exactly the kind of treatment female artists have had to endure for years, but with JBJ the tables were turned due to his magnetism.

THE REVIEWS & COMMERCIAL RECEPTION

Slippery When Wet became the first hard rock album to have three Top 10 singles in the *Billboard* Hit 100: "You Give Love A Bad Name" and "Livin' On A Prayer" both hit Number 1 and "Wanted Dead Or Alive" reached Number 7. And not only did the album itself get to Number 1 in the Billboard 200 album charts but it stayed there proudly for eight weeks and a staggering 38 weeks inside the Top 5.

Such was the album's staying power that, despite being released in the summer of 1986 in the US, it was actually the bestselling album of 1987. This is presumably due in part to the success of the singles released from the album prompting consumers to want to find out more about the band's music. In fact, in the year of its release, the album only hit the number one spot in the US for one week at the end of October.

However, at the end of January 1987, Bon Jovi knocked fellow New Jerseysian Bruce Springsteen and his Live 1975-'85 off the top spot. The band were top of the rock until the end of February when the Beastie Boys replaced them with *Licenced To Ill*. Other notable number one albums that year were *Whitney* by Whitney Houston (which was released in 1985, but didn't hit the top spot until 1986 and again in 1987), *The Joshua Tree* from U2, Michael Jackson's *Bad* and Springsteen's *Tunnel Of Love*. Apart from those, the only other records to get to number one were both soundtracks – *La Bamba* and *Dirty Dancing*.

What about the album's success in the UK? Well, it only peaked at Number 6 but it did spend over a hundred weeks in the Top 25, with 23 weeks in the Top 20. For the statisticians amongst you, 1987 saw 23 different albums hit the number one spot in the UK compared to only nine in the US. It would appear that the larger population of the US means that albums have more longevity as people buy them over longer time periods, whereas in the UK they come and go much quicker.

The album remains Bon Jovi's bestselling work in both the USA and UK. In other countries, *Slippery When Wet* hit the top spot in Australia, Canada, Finland, New Zealand, Norway and Switzerland, and it also made it to the top 15 in Germany, Japan, Sweden and the Netherlands.

However, with all the success they'd achieved off the back of *Slippery When Wet* the band found themselves pigeon-holed in the over-saturated hair metal market. Sambora told *JoyZine*'s Anne Raso years after the album came out: "We're certainly not heavy metal, and we're certainly not pussy rock! What we tried to do is just make a Bon Jovi album. It's appealing to all kinds of people because it's powerful and the songs are good. Rock 'n' roll – and, hopefully, Bon Jovi music – is something that a lot of people can get into. It's one of the most popular forms of music. You know, I guess some people are hung up on labels. I listen to all kinds of music; I'm not hung up on one type. That's something that always pissed me off in the past that kids don't open up their heads and listen to everything."

It was obvious – even more so now, with the benefit of hindsight and quarter of a century later – that the band and their team were aiming for a commercial album; perhaps far more commercial than the hair and glam metal bands that were popular on the West Coast. It was a trend that Bon Jovi wanted to distance themselves from, though they wouldn't properly do that until the early '90s with *Keep The Faith*.

The critical reception was less enthusiastic than the commercial one, but they still won some critics over to their side. The highbrow critics of music journalism's so called elite have never understood the appeal of melodic rock, and have derided and deplored it over the years, yet critics in the know love this style of music and *Slippery When Wet* is up there with the best of them. Therefore it comes as a surprise to learn that in his famed *Consumer Guide Reviews*, Robert Christgau (the self-proclaimed "Dean of American Rock Critics") declared: "Sure seven million teenagers can be wrong, but their assent is not without a certain documentary satisfaction. Yes, it proves that youth rebellion is toothless enough to simulate and market. But who the hell thought youth was dangerous in the current vacuum? Would you have preferred the band market patriotism? And are you really immune to 'Livin' On A Prayer'? B -"

Jimmy Guterman was not exactly enthused in his review of the album, published in *Rolling Stone*. Guterman wrote, "On *Slippery When Wet*, Bon

Jovi sounds like bad fourth-generation metal, a smudgy Xerox of Quiet Riot." Ouch!

In 1998, JBJ did admit to Ingrid Sischy of New York's *Interview Magazine* that he became full of himself after the success of the album: "Sure, during *Slippery* and *New Jersey*. And a lot of that arrogance, in retrospect, was out of fear of the success not being there forever. People who have to tell you how successful they are aren't really successful. That's something I learned sweeping floors at this recording studio called the Power Station. Mediocre stars were the biggest pricks, and the big stars were the ones who came in and said: 'How're those demos going? Keep pushing, you'll get it. It'll happen for you.'"

7
THE SLIPPERY WHEN WET TOUR

In 2001, JBJ spoke to *VH-1.com* about how the Bon Jovi audience had changed over the years: "They're there to see us and challenge us to surprise them with a great show. In the beginning we were eager to prove that we were different than our peers, but that took time and persistence. *Slippery* began the true Bon Jovi era."

The *Slippery When Wet* Tour was a mammoth undertaking for the Jersey boys. Sure, they had two previous albums under their collective belts and were not novices on the live circuit, but they probably didn't realize at the start of the tour in 1986 just how gruelling it would be as they went into 1987. However, it must be said that they would perform an even bigger road jaunt with the New Jersey Syndicate Tour, beginning in 1988.

It was the band's first major world tour, on which they would visit some faraway places that they had not yet been to, such as Australia and parts of Europe.

"We started touring before the record was even close to being out," JBJ told VH-1 in 2002. "I said: 'Let's open for the Cars or Bryan Adams.' Our manager Doc McGhee said: 'No. We're going out with the Scorpions and Judas Priest. We're going out with guys that have had a whole lot of records and a fanbase that isn't fickle and they're going to learn to like you.' That was like a kick in the teeth. We had to learn fast because they were good, tight rock bands."

THE *SLIPPERY WHEN WET* TOUR

Ain't that the truth?

Bon Jovi kicked off the first leg of the tour with an eight date visit to Canada – beginning 14 July in their old stomping ground of Vancouver – playing support to Judas Priest on their Turbo Tour (also dubbed the Fuel For Life Tour). Priest were at the height of their success in North America, playing big venues and championing themselves as the "Metal Gods".

Jonathan Valen – who at the time was on tour with Judas Priest as their controversial second drummer – remembers: "Bon Jovi was probably the most professional support band I encountered during that period. The crew all wore custom shirts with embroidered flags of different countries on them. We had toured with them through Canada when *Slippery When Wet* hit the charts and the rest is history. We knew they were going on to greatness. Those boys deserve all the success they achieved."

Bon Jovi then flew to Japan for the second leg of the tour, playing nine headlining shows all over the country from Nagoya on 11 August to Sapporo on 25 August. There is a story from Japan that sums up why Bon Jovi were always going to succeed. When they played the legendary Budokan in Tokyo, they hadn't sold all the tickets. JBJ sprang into action doing all the publicity he could for the show, even offering punters their money back if they weren't satisfied. Now that's commitment for you.

The band flew over to the UK on 7 November for a major 23 date tour of Europe, beginning in Bradford and winding up in Helsinki on 8 December. Support came from the excellent British melodic rock band, FM.

FM's drummer, Pete Jupp, recalls, "The main thing was it was a really exciting time, it was just when they'd absolutely exploded worldwide. They treated us absolutely brilliantly on the tour; we couldn't have asked for anything more. It's true. They were great. I remember one night, I think their soundcheck had overrun, and the old bass player Alec [John Such] was there saying, 'No, No, hold the doors, hold the doors. Let them [FM] do a quick soundcheck.' They were brilliant. I remember when we did Bradford Queen's Hall; that was the first time I'd experienced someone screaming at us. The whole tour was brilliant. We'd done a lot of other tours with other people but they couldn't have treated us any better … a really nice bunch of guys."

Moving on, Bon Jovi played a series of shows in London, which was interrupted by two nights in Liverpool and Stoke On Trent on November 20 and November 21, respectively. Those shows proved that the band's fanbase was quickly getting bigger as a result of the album's mass popularity.

Writer John Tucker recounts attending the first show on 17 November. He penned a personal review right after witnessing the band in action way back when:

> Almost overnight, Bon Jovi have become a household name in Britain, and it's doubtful whether the albums and tours of the previous two years had done anything to prepare the band for the adulation they've received since their

arrival here. Two hit singles have paved the way for TV appearances and tabloid coverage, which in turn have boosted sales of *Slippery When Wet* and turned what may have been a perfunctory UK tour into a massive sold out success.

Tonight was the first of four - count 'em! - nights at Hammersmith Odeon, and although it's great to see a band getting the acclaim it richly deserves, one glance around the audience showed it to be mainly composed of recent converts of the *Slippery* ... kind; and success built on singles can be short lived as the record buying public move swiftly on to the next 'in' thing. So it came as no surprise that the set featured more songs from the new album than from its two predecessors combined, and for the biggest applause of the night to go to the two singles "You Give Love A Bad Name" and "Livin' On A Prayer". But from the opening strains of "Raise Your Hands" to the last few bars of a rocked up "Get Ready", Jon Bon Jovi had the capacity crowd in the palm of his hand, a puppet master pulling the strings of four thousand eager marionettes. The set itself drew largely on the best of the new album supported by three old favourites apiece from the band's self-titled debut and *7800° Fahrenheit*, the only personal low spots being the all-too-bland "Silent Night" and the horrendous "Wild In The Streets".

As ever though, the best was saved till last, the first encore producing a soul searching rendition of "Wanted Dead Or Alive'" - perhaps the finest showcase of the band's songwriting abilities - and a cover of Thin Lizzy's "The Boys Are Back In Town" as a tribute to Phil Lynott R.I.P. Called back for more, Bon Jovi - complete with brass trio - ripped through the excellent "Social Disease" and a lively version of the otherwise ordinary "Get Ready". It was a great night, believe me.

After winding up the UK tour where it began, in Bradford, they flew to the Netherlands for a show in Arnhem, Holland on 27 November. Support for many of the European dates came from Queensrÿche. The European leg of the tour finished in Helsinki on 8 December.

Was there time for a Christmas break? Hell no! Bon Jovi kicked off the fourth leg of the tour in Baltimore on 19 December. Throughout the North American leg many of the shows saw Bon Jovi supported by the glam rockers Cinderella. Hailing from Philadelphia, Cinderella got

LET IT ROCK

their major break courtesy of Jon Bon Jovi who saw them play at Philly's Empire Rock Club. He was so impressed he brought them to the attention of Bon Jovi's then A&R man Derek Shulman, who got them a deal with Mercury in 1985. Cinderella went on to sell over twenty million albums and are still going strong to this day.

The North American leg was a massive undertaking as the band performed 149 live shows. They finished with two nights at Uniondale in New York on 9 and 10 August 1987. After the North American leg wound up, the band flew back to England for a headlining spot on the famed Monsters Of Rock festival at Castle Donington on 22 August. When you consider that also on the bill were Dio, Anthrax, Metallica, W.A.S.P. and Cinderella you can see how far the band had come to be top of the shop over such acts as Dio, Metallica and Anthrax.

Here's Bon Jovi's set list from the Monsters Of Rock show: They opened with an extended version of "Pink Flamingos". This is a scene setter to get the audience expectation to fever pitch and must take a lot of nerve on David Bryan's part. Imagine - it's the opening number, the nerves are there and you have to do an organ solo in front of thousands of people. Even if you play it every night, it must still be a challenge. It goes into "Raise Your Hands", "I'd Die For You", "Tokyo Road", "You Give Love A Bad Name", "Wild In The Streets", Buddy Holly's "Not Fade Away", "Never Say Goodbye", "Livin' On A Prayer", "Let It Rock", "Get Ready", "Runaway", "Wanted Dead Or Alive", Mentor Williams' much covered "Drift Away", Creedence Clearwater Revival's "Travelin' Band" and Grand Funk Railroad's "We're An American Band".

The fifth and penultimate leg of this gargantuan tour was in Australia, which commenced in Melbourne on 5 September and finished in Sydney on 18 September. Finally, the band played in Japan (from 24 September to 7 October) before finishing with three shows in Honolulu, Hawaii on 15, 16, 17 October. Virtually the whole of 1987 was spent on tour, which certainly helped the band in terms of raising their profile with thousands of new fans.

THE *SLIPPERY WHEN WET* TOUR

Sambora and Such rock out at the Meadowlands Arena, NJ, New Year's Eve 1986. (*Bob Leafe / Frank White Agency*)

Bon Jovi played a staggering 206 shows in total, with 24 shows in Europe, 149 in North America, twenty in East Asia and thirteen in Australia, giving them stamps in their passports from countries they could never have dreamed of visiting a few short years ago.

As with most bands, Bon Jovi shook up the set list and didn't play the same songs throughout the whole tour, but here's an example of what they played on some nights: "Pink Flamingos", "Raise Your Hands", "Breakout", "I'd Die For You", "Tokyo Road", "You Give Love A Bad Name", "Wild In The Streets", "Silent Night", "Livin' On A Prayer", "Let It Rock", (Guitar Solo/Drum Solo), "In And Out Of Love" and "Runaway" with an encore of "Wanted Dead Or Alive", "Drift Away" and finally, "Get Ready".

LET IT ROCK

Photographer Mark Weiss remembers the euphoria surrounding the band. "Probably the *Slippery* era," he says when asked about his most memorable experience of working with the band, "all the videos, going to Japan and South America, around the world. At that time they were flying on these little private planes and all that, but they were definitely a band. It was five people. The band thought it was five people. I think in years to come it was not five people anymore, it was Jon. He was the guy who called the shots ... Jon knows what he's doing. I think Jon is a smart guy and he's got a lot more plans for the future. He's on the right track for sure. Every decade of music there's a couple of them that come out like Bon Jovi ... there's definitely one band that makes it through. And they were one of the ones that made it through for whatever reason. The timing, the decisions."

The *Slippery When Wet* Tour marked the beginning of Bon Jovi's status as one of the world's leading live rock bands. To this day, Bon Jovi remain so; constantly breaking record attendances as well as topping the lists of the most profitable live acts of the year.

"When [the *Slippery When Wet*] tour ended, ten months later, we had another album written and recorded, and we were back in Ireland starting the tour," JBJ told Allison Stewart of *CDNow* in 2001. "Someone at a press conference in Ireland said to me, 'What are you doing here?' And at the time, I thought, What a stupid question – we're starting a tour; we're playing tonight. It took me a couple years to realize that that was the most intelligent, deep question the guy could have asked me, and he was right. We should have stopped, just enjoyed the moment. Went home. Instead of being out there like a bunch of young punk prizefighters. Like, 'Come on! Anybody else? What do you want, another No. 1 single? You got it. Another one? All right, fine: ... We were on fire. When that tour was over, my brain was liquid."

REFLECTIONS ON THE TOUR

Phil Ashcroft (*Fireworks: The Melodic Rock Magazine*): "I remember the sound being good and the band being much more confident than the previous tour – where I thought they were overshadowed by Lee Aaron (in my humble opinion). They had an intro tape and bigger lights, and Jon appeared behind a venetian blind-like screen above the drum riser as they opened with 'Raise Your Hands'. The set was all killer, no filler and they had quite a few big songs by that point, with 'Tokyo Road', 'Breakout', 'You Give Love A Bad Name', 'Livin' On A Prayer', 'In And Out Of Love', 'Runaway' and 'Wanted Dead Or Alive' being particularly effective. It was a high energy set, 'Silent Night' being the only ballad, and they ended the set with 'The Boys Are Back In Town'. It was also the first time I noticed just how good a singer Richie Sambora was, with an almost a cappella version of 'Drift Away' starting an encore that also included 'Get Ready', which I thought at the time was one of their weaker songs and a disappointing closer. It was obvious that they were on their way to the next level, and venues like Liverpool's Royal Court – which had been booked six months previous – were sell outs and just weren't big enough to hold them. It was their last time in the theatres, the next time they came over would be for the Donington Monsters Of Rock and multiple nights in the big indoor arenas."

Andreas Carlsson (Songwriter/Bon Jovi Collaborator): "I saw Bon Jovi in the '80s opening for KISS in Sweden; I was always a big fan. *Slippery When Wet* is probably one of the best rock albums ever made, and Jon is the ultimate front man. Watching him closely onstage is a treat."

Rob Evans (*Powerplay*): "Having witnessed the fledgling Bon Jovi as the support act on the KISS Animalize Tour of the UK in 1984, and a superb headline gig a year later at the Manchester Apollo, it was obvious from the outset that they were always destined for stardom. However I don't think

LET IT ROCK

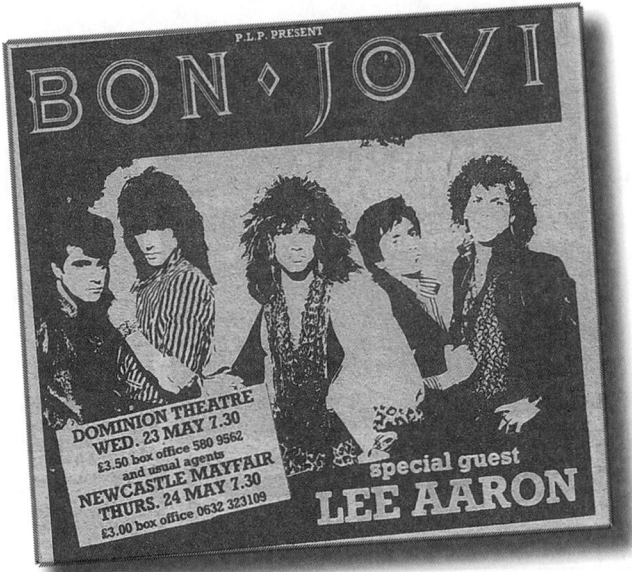

Advert for the first headlining tour in 1985. Bon Jovi would quickly progress to larger venues.

that anyone could have predicted just how big a global phenomenon they would turn into.

To say that *Slippery When Wet* was the catalyst that kick started this phenomenon would be a massive understatement. It propelled them to the top at such an alarming rate that I'm sure the band didn't have time to catch their breath. The album itself is an infectious mix of chart potential and hard rock savvy that saw main songwriters Jon Bon Jovi and Richie Sambora joining Desmond Child to create an album that was very nearly perfect. The hard core AOR cognoscenti that embraced them on their debut album had to face the fact that their fave cult band of the time was waving them goodbye as their hurtled down the runway marked fame, and it was hard to let them go.

On the subsequent tour, I managed to catch them at the Manchester Apollo, the Liverpool Royal Court and Hanley Victoria Halls and I

THE *SLIPPERY WHEN WET* TOUR

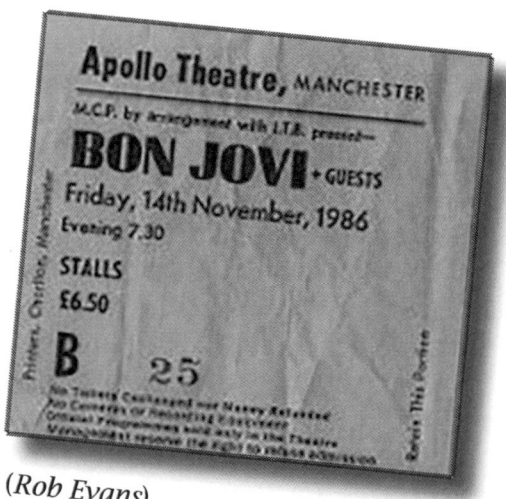

(*Rob Evans*)

witnessed a band on fire, a band that over the course of three albums had gone from the slightly awkward one that supported KISS, into a slick, polished act that could grace any stage with aplomb. In Jon Bon Jovi they had a front man who gave an abject lesson in stagecraft every night.

Of course, the pinnacle of this album and its subsequent tour would be the band's headline slot at the following year's Monsters Of Rock show at Donington Park. In front of 70,000 fans they had well and truly arrived and gave a performance that was both captivating and mesmerizing in equal amounts. With a supporting cast that included the likes of Cinderella, W.A.S.P., Anthrax, Metallica and Dio, Bon Jovi easily gave the best performance on this wet dreary day. As they say, the rest is history."

Jason Ritchie (*Get Ready To Rock.com*): "I saw them in 1987 at the Victoria Hall, Hanley on the *Slippery When Wet* Tour (hands up who remembers the T-shirts with the scantily clad lady on them?) and it was a good turnout. Again, the band were on fire and they were certainly more confident on stage, with Jon Bon Jovi and Richie Sambora both running all over the stage and working the crowd. 'Livin' On A Prayer' brought the house down and the good thing about a Bon Jovi gig back then was that they attracted a healthy quota of females. This was the last hall-sized tour of the UK, as next time they came back they were into the arenas. I am always glad I saw them in a smaller venue like the Victoria Hall as the band really thrived off the closeness of the audience and their response to the music."

Derek Shulman: "I attended so many shows they become blurred. However, I think that some of the earliest UK and European shows were the best ones. Mainly because I saw how the band were able to hit a new audience and foreign city and be totally unafraid of working and building their following city by city, country by country. *Slippery When Wet* was a culmination of incredible hard work from the management, the company, but most importantly the band over four-five years of development and ultimately major record sales, finally."

Jeb Wright (*Classic Rock Revisited.com*): "I was pumped to see the Scorpions on the Love At First Sting Tour in Wichita, Kansas. After all, they are one of my favourite bands. Opening up for the Scorps were a band I had never heard of … Bon Jovi. I didn't even know what a Bon Jovi was and must admit that I was more interested in drinking beer and looking at girls than seeing the opening act. When the lights went down, however, a few facts became clear. First off, the guitar player was a badass. He could flat out jam. The other thing that caught my eye was the fact that the lead singer had big '80s hair and looked a lot better than most of the girls I had been scoping out. The music was more pop metal than I was used to but at the end of each song every girl in the audience screamed like they were watching The Beatles. I turned and looked to my friend and said: 'Dude, hard rock is changing.' Boy was I right. Bon Jovi went on to be one of the biggest bands of all time. The only song I recognized when they played that night was 'Runaway'. But I could tell I was witnessing the start of something special."

8
REFLECTIONS ON *SLIPPERY WHEN WET* – WHAT THE ROCK WRITERS THINK

So what do rock critics and reviewers think of the album as it stands over 25 years later? I spoke to several rock experts about the legacy of Slippery When Wet ...

Bailey Brothers (Broadcasters/journalists): "This was a definitive moment in rock history because for once rock was mainstream on national radio, TV and tabloid news. The sales were phenomenal, over 12 million and probably going on to achieve 30 million sales worldwide which is amazing in any genre, but in rock it was groundbreaking. Bon Jovi were like the Osmonds of rock, attracting seasoned rock fans and teeny boppers alike. All the labels wanted the next Bon Jovi, so it opened the door for many acts. Others would say it was the time when rock went pop and British bands, especially, abandoned their blues roots for a more commercial approach. The unsung heroes of that album are Desmond Child, Bob Rock and Bruce Fairbairn. At the end of the day Jovi, Sambora

LET IT ROCK

and Child wrote what proved to be rock anthems. The Bailey Brothers felt the *SWW* wave first hand as every club we played at the dance floor would be crammed full with young fans rockin' to 'Livin' On A Prayer' and 'You Give Love A Bad Name' written by Jovi, Sambora and Child. Fairbairn and Child went on to work with Aerosmith on the *Permanent Vacation* album; another really credible release. A few years earlier we were trying to drag the UK fans on the dance floor to 'Runaway' from Bon Jovi. We had the pleasure of being on the same Monsters Of Rock bill as Bon Jovi and hung with them a few times during their rise to fame and they were just as cool offstage. One thing that should not be over looked is that Bon Jovi are a kick ass live rock 'n' roll band, it's one thing recording an album with as many takes as is required to make a perfect recording, but well before SWW Jovi had earned a reputation as a cool live act. Jon Bon Jovi has a great work ethic and professionalism, it's to his credit he didn't just go solo with a bunch of session musicians. Bon Jovi became a worldwide stadium band by the end of this tour and remains a stadium band today and that is an amazing feat. The album had much more substance than the poppy songs they are famed for; 'Wanted Dead Or Alive' is a cool tune but then Sambora and Jovi are a great writing partnership and *Slippery When Wet* is an album they should always be proud of. Whitesnake's *1987* and *Hysteria* from Def Leppard (released in 1987) from a rock fans point of view may be more appealing but on a commercial level Jovi and SWW were untouchable."

Neil Jeffries (Author of *Bon Jovi: A Biography*): "You could argue it's become unfashionable, and even a mild embarrassment to many of those who bought it first time around, but there's no denying *Slippery When Wet* was an important record that still resonates today. It's one of those rare albums that stands as a template for a whole genre. Bon Jovi – to their credit – looked to move on with *New Jersey* and never opted for a cop out remake, but plenty of bands did. And today, with the resurgence in AOR music around the world, bands old and new are still using it as a reference point. The songs and sound of *Slippery* have influenced countless bands from Scandinavia and Western Europe, and in the American heartland of radio rock the mark of the album is still audible in 2011 releases by bands as diverse as House Of Lords and Whitesnake."

Joe Matera (*Ultimate-Guitar.com*): "*Slippery When Wet* is one of those rare albums that have managed to transcend the boundaries of time and the generational gap. Even today, walk into any pub or club and you're sure to hear either 'Livin' On A Prayer' or 'Wanted Dead Or Alive' being played by either a jukebox or a band, with the audience, many of whom weren't even born the first time the album came out, singing along to all the words. Having become Bon Jovi's calling card, it is also the benchmark upon which everything produced by the band since has been judged. Its glossy production brought all the right elements of Bon Jovi's live sound and energy into the mix, while the group's rough-around-the-edges sound from its previous two albums has finally been given a refined spit and polish. The group's bestselling album, it shot Bon Jovi to super stardom and into the annals of rock history, forever finding an audience on a mass scale. Its core themes striking at the heart of everyday common people with tracks such as 'Livin' On A Prayer', 'I'd Die For You' and 'Never Say Goodbye'. The album also boasts one of the best marriages of electric and acoustic ever committed to tape via the outlaw paen of 'Wanted Dead Or Alive', while 'You Give Love A Bad Name' cleverly turns a lover's angst into a celebratory party anthem. All in all, *Slippery When Wet* defines Bon Jovi the band and who they were yesterday and who they are today. And, with *Slippery When Wet*, the last bastion of '80s hair metal would ride out the wave before the onslaught of grunge."

Dean Pedley (*Fireworks: The Melodic Rock Magazine*): "Just like his childhood hero, Bruce Springsteen, record number three was the one as far as the career trajectory of Jon Bon Jovi was concerned. Without the resultant mega-sales for both the album and its various singles, the future might well have turned out very differently for the boy from New

LET IT ROCK

Jersey, with stadiums, private jets and sports team ownership replaced by annual treks around the state fair circuit. What *Slippery When Wet* also has in common with *Born To Run*, aside from being regarded as the jewel in the back catalogue, is the all important factor of 'timing' – being unquestionably the right record for the moment.

A quarter of a century on, 'Livin' On A Prayer', 'Wanted Dead Or Alive' and 'You Give Love A Bad Name' remain staples of rock nights around the globe and whilst they may suffer from over-familiarity, each contains that irresistible combination of melody and magic that was notably lacking on *7800° Fahrenheit*. 'Let It Rock' provides the perfect opening number both on record and on stage, building the mood to a resounding crescendo. Dig deeper and 'I'd Die For You', 'Wild In The Streets' and 'Raise Your Hands' are fist-pumping, crowd-pleasing anthems that grab the listener within the first ten seconds and maintain a vice-like grip throughout each and every verse, chorus and solo. Even 'Without Love' and 'Social Disease', the nearest to what could be classified as 'filler', are solid enough and deserving of their place in the final running order. Finally, 'Never Say Goodbye' goes to prove that no classic album can ever be complete without a reflective, lighters-in-the-air power ballad of love lost and found.

Their songwriting may have matured, but Bon Jovi would never again sound as exciting, fresh or vital as they did on *Slippery* and, just like Born To Run, it remains one of the most vibrant and compelling 30-odd minutes in the annals of rock."

Jason Ritchie (*Get Ready to Rock.com*): "I first became a fan of Bon Jovi after seeing them at Monsters Of Rock in 1985 on their UK debut touring the *7800° Fahrenheit* album. I thought this was a pretty good album until their next release, *Slippery When Wet*. Rushing back from my local record shop with a cassette copy of the new album, from the first listen to the keyboard intro to 'Let It Rock' I knew that this was going to be a good listen and then some. In fact only one song, 'Social Disease' still fails to hit the spot for me all these years later.

REFLECTIONS ON *SLIPPERY WHEN WET*

Every song on here could have been released as a single and been a hit, such is the strength of the songs and their choruses. 'You Give Love A Bad Name', 'Wanted Dead Or Alive' and 'Livin' On A Prayer' worked well when heard live on the 1986 tour. But a song like 'Raise Your Hands' was made for the live arena and I can still recall the sold out crowd going wild at the Victoria Hall, Hanley back in 1986. The programme cover also sticks in the mind as well as it featured the rejected album cover artwork featuring a lady in a tight, wet t-shirt ... err I'd better leave it there.

The follow up, New Jersey, was another strong album but lacked the real impact of *Slippery When Wet*, which summed up the mid/late '80s hair metal music and quite rightly became one of the biggest selling albums of the decade (it was the bestselling album in the US for 1987). They have never bettered this album in my view, but at least they can say unlike many bands they have a classic album like this in their catalogue.

Playing it now the songs still sound fresh and although I am a lapsed fan of the band now – the last album I really enjoyed was 2000's *Crush* – I still play *Slippery When Wet* and enjoy it every time ..."

Steven Rosen (Rock Journalist/Author): "It is very easy to explain why *Slippery When Wet* blew Bon Jovi up: songs. The songs brought together the elusive pieces of pumping rock rhythms and melodic vocals and married them perfectly under the masterful gaze of producer Bruce Fairbairn. Guitarist Richie Sambora and singer Jon Bon Jovi realized their own limitations as songwriters and reached out to Desmond Child for input. He helped them co-write 'You Give Love A Bad Name' and 'Livin' On A Prayer', two songs that would go on to become mainstays of the New Jersey band's live performances. Funny though, because Jon Bon Jovi almost made the mistake of his life.

"Livin' On A Prayer' sort of changed the way rock radio worked,' Jon described to this writer. 'If A&R guys had listened to me, we would have never even done that song. That shows you what I know. I just didn't think it was a very good song.'

LET IT ROCK

He was wrong, of course, and based on the strength of that song and several other monster singles, the album would go on to sell more than 28 million copies. But let's not overlook the value of a pretty face and cool hair. Both Jon and Richie Sambora were amazing looking rock musicians and the fact they looked like pinups certainly fuelled the fires of female fans around the world.

But when it was all said and done, the songs were everything. In fact, they've never created music with that kind of mass appeal since. Bon Jovi had some classically brilliant songs and a lot of filler – it just goes to show you that a handful of masterpieces can make up for a whole lot of ordinary.

'It was the songwriting that made the leap, really,' Sambora explained to me. This band was an amazing live unit so all we really needed was the songs and a great producer, which we did get with Bruce Fairbairn and a star engineer by the name of Bob Rock. I said: 'Yeah, we got it, man, we're definitely gonna go double platinum on this.' Des was a part of that record also, but Jon and I had written 'Wanted Dead Or Alive' and 'Never Say Goodbye' and we were on a roll. We started to find out what this band was about.'"

Kimmo Toivonen (*Rock United.com*): "According to IFPI, Bon Jovi's *Slippery When Wet* has sold around 73,000 copies in Finland. Strangely enough, they only got the Platinum award for the album in 1990. By today's standards, 73,000 sold albums would mean triple-platinum.

In 1986, Bon Jovi were virtually unknown in Finland, but within a few weeks they conquered the country. And they did it without having to set foot here. It all started with their 'You Give Love A Bad Name' video being shown on the popular TV show *HITTIMITTARI (Hit Meter)*, and soon they were everywhere – TV, radio, magazines. I soon got myself the album or most likely a cassette copy of it, and listened to it almost religiously. It made me a fan of the band, a fan of Desmond Child and even a fan of the 'look' – I let my hair grow long, ripped my jeans and so on. Thankfully the band had a rather down-to-earth glam rock look that was easier to imitate on a shoestring budget than that of Poison and the likes. Besides, I was never interested in make up or women's clothing ...

SWW has never really been my all-time favourite album, but the best tracks of it are among my all-time favourite songs. '... Bad Name,' 'Livin' On A Prayer' and 'I'd Die For You' are still capable of making shivers go down my spine, even though I've heard each one of them about a million times. On the other hand, I've never really warmed up to 'Social Disease' or the sugary 'Never Say Goodbye.' Quite why they left off 'Edge Of A Broken Heart' from the album I really can't understand, that should've been one of the singles.

A few weeks ago I was at a Bon Jovi concert, and they ended their set with '... Prayer' and 40,000 people were singing along. Those damn shivers were running up and down, and I thought to myself that if there ever was a 'perfect song', this was it. After 25 years, that song can almost make a grown man cry ... instead of crying, I just shouted 'WHOOOOA, We're halfway there ...'"

Just so nobody can accuse us of a one sided account, here is the alternative view on Bon Jovi from my old pal Jeb Wright (*Classic Rock Revisited*): "O.K., for starters I have no idea why the author of this book would want an essay by me on the subject of Bon Jovi's *Slippery When Wet* album. Neil Daniels knows me personally and knows how I feel about this subject. Sure, I'm a rock and roll expert and all, but, when it comes to Bon Jovi, I just can't separate my feelings, mainly hatred, from the fact that this is perhaps one of the most beloved albums of the 1980s.

Neil knows that I would rather be stripped naked, covered in honey and fire ants and hung from a meat hook above an open flame, all the while being forced to listen to Celine Dion, than I would have any of my senses be subjected to anything Bon Jovi has ever done. You see, I, Jeb Wright, blame none other than Jon Bon Jovi for ruining hard rock and heavy metal and for ushering in hairspray rock to the masses. He single handedly made it O.K. for Frat boys to like hard rock and for that alone I just can't forgive him. Sure, he brought more tittie flashes to

LET IT ROCK

rock concerts but at what cost? I mean, he scores points for that and all but when preppie girls started going to metal concerts it just seemed so wrong ... so ... dirty...

Slippery When Wet. Sure, the album sold ten bazillion copies and every female that went to high school in 1986 went moist every time she looked at a picture of Mr Fluffy Hair, with his good looks and boyish smile. The guy has it going on but that is no reason to ruin the hard rock culture that I loved.

Now, rock photographer Mark 'Weissguy' Weiss had the right idea when he photographed a big-titted girl in a wet t-shirt for the original album cover. Nothing says rock and roll like big tits and hard nipples on a hot chick. Hell, if he'd kept this cover then I might have even become a fan!

O.K., enough of my bellyaching. I believe I have made my point. I have to admit – begrudgingly, mind you – that I do understand what all the hubbub about this album is about. I mean, come on, the guy is handsome, can sing, has a talented band behind him and has an uncanny ability to create songs full of pop hooks and sweet lyrics that will melt the heart of the most frigid woman in the world. It is the fact that he does this all under the guise of hard rock that pricks me in the ass.

As much as I detest Celine Dion and that Elton John song about the Lion King, I have to admit it is pop music made for the large audience of musically retarded individuals in the world. I think Bon Jovi is pop music hidden behind hair spray, expensive leather pants and spandex. He did the same thing when he went country; only then it was pop music hid behind cowboy hats, boots and cow poop.

Hell, he's got a good gig going on. He can read this article, wipe his butt with it and laugh all the way to the bank while I am stuck eating a Nathan's hot dog from a street vendor, counting the change out of the cup holder in my car, hoping to scratch enough change together to buy a small Coke. I get it. He's rich, wildly popular, talented and full of business savvy.

If truth be told there is one and only one song of JBJ's that I can stomach and maybe, just maybe, when no one is around me that I sort of like and might even, on occasion, play loudly. I even learned the guitar part. 'Wanted Dead Or Alive' is a damn good song. And, while I don't like the other tunes on *Slippery When Wet*, I again, will swallow that stomach acid back down and admit I can see why others do. 'Raise Your Hands', 'Wild In The Street' and 'I'd Die For You' all have that 'it' factor that makes a great pop song a great pop song - and these are not even the big hits on the album. 'Livin' On A Prayer' even has an apostrophe instead of a lower case 'g' making it look cool. The song shows Jon has some pipes and that his band can, and I hate to say this, rock out!

This brings me to the song that made the biggest impact on the album, 'You Give Love A Bad Name'. Again, I can see why people love it. In the world of pop rock this is absolutely 100% perfection. There is nothing in this song that is not exactly where it is supposed to be. Every guitar note in the solo is perfect, every note sung is perfect and the song ebbs and flows with perfect timing and effect. Why then does it make my lower intestine fill with diarrhea? I don't know why but it just does. Perhaps I am allergic to Jon Bon Jovi, yet I can still see why someone who is not allergic to him might like him, much the same way someone who is lactose intolerant and can't handle milk understands the joy others find in a simple milkshake.

The bottom line here is that what I think really does not matter. The world will not stop spinning just because I do not like his music. World peace will still elude us and there will still be war in the Middle East after you're finished reading this essay. And, worst of all, people will continue to love *Slippery When Wet*. So, it is with a sigh and great trepidation that I must end this article by saying that if you like this album, then so be it. I understand why, because it is well written, well executed, well produced and well polished. It shines. I get it. Still, I wish they would have left the tits.

So, Neil, there you have it. I have gotten this off my chest and I must admit I feel better ... so thank you for this opportunity. Now, if I could only get that damn song, 'Livin' On A Prayer', out of my fucking head!"

9
THE SLIPPERY WHEN WET TEAM

The following list offers potted histories of the key personnel behind the making and legacy of Slippery When Wet. *Without these guys, the album and tour would perhaps not have been so successful ...*

RAY BROWN
Ray Brown is universally known as one of rock's most successful and revered fashion designers. In the 1980s, he was rock's most sought after designer working with the biggest bands in the business, including Black Sabbath, Judas Priest, Mötley Crüe, Ozzy Osbourne and Whitesnake. He was the "go-to guy" in LA when it came to rock fashion. He also tailored togs for the weddings of Jon Bon Jovi, Vince Neil and John Mellencamp. As well as working with Richie Sambora on his first solo tour, Brown designed clothes for Bon Jovi for over a decade.

Brown first hooked up with them at the time of *Slippery When Wet*. He remembers, "The one thing I do remember about them was: everything was badass. That's how they'd describe their clothing; everything was bad or badass. I had a really large workshop; I would just buy fabric that I saw that I liked and they would just pick fabric and just say, 'Make a badass coat out of this or make a badass coat out of that.' They did contribute to a lot of the designs but most guys that are in bands, they have an idea of how they wanna look on stage so it's just a matter of interpreting it for them. A lot of the time, especially with Richie, it was like 'Make me a badass white coat or make me a badass purple coat.'"

How did Brown find working with the band during that period? "They were very open," he says. "Basically, they would just pick fabric or just describe something they wanted and just get me to interpret it. They were obviously happy because it went on for a very long time. One of the coats that I made for Jon – that one with the skulls on it, the long patchwork coat – he ended up giving away to the Smithsonian Museum in New York."

DESMOND CHILD

Probably one of the most respected songwriters in rock, Desmond Child is best known for his work with Meat Loaf, Aerosmith, Scorpions, Alice Cooper, Poison, Cher, and Michael Bolton. He also co-wrote the KISS classic "I Was Made For Loving You" with Paul Stanley from the Dynasty album. Since writing with Bon Jovi on the *Slippery When Wet* album, Desmond Child has worked extensively with the band: he co-produced 2002's *Bounce* and was executive producer for 2005's *Have A Nice Day* and 2007's *Lost Highway*. He also had some creative input on Jon's first proper solo album, *Destination Anywhere*, co-producing the track "Ugly" with Eric Bazilian.

BRUCE FAIRBAIRN

Aside from his work with Bon Jovi, the late Canadian rock producer Bruce Fairbairn's credits include Aerosmith, Loverboy, KISS, AC/DC, Chicago, INXS, Dan Reed Network and Blue Öyster Cult. Bon Jovi were so pleased with Fairbairn's production of *Slippery When Wet* that he was invited back to produce 1988's *New Jersey*, an equally successful and now classic album. It was recorded over a three month period in early 1988 at Fairbairn's Little Mountain Sound Studios in Vancouver. He also produced the 1999 single "Real Life", which was crafted specifically for the movie *EdTV*. Fairbairn died on 17 May 1999 at his home in Vancouver. He was just 49 years old and the cause of death remains unknown. In 2000, the Canadian Music Hall Of Fame gave him a posthumous award.

BOB ROCK
Bob Rock was initially Bruce Fairbairn's protégé and would later find enormous success as a record producer in his own right. His credits as either as a producer, engineer or mixer include Metallica, Mötley Crüe, David Lee Roth, Skid Row, Bryan Adams, The Cult, Black N' Blue, Kingdom Come, Survivor, Krokus, and Aerosmith. He is also a musician and played bass on Metallica's 2003 album *St. Anger*. After working with Bon Jovi on *Slippery When Wet*, Rock also engineered 1988s New Jersey and produced Keep The Faith in 1992, which marked a major shift in the band's musical direction.

MARK WEISS
Though some of his best and most popular work is with Bon Jovi, Mark Weiss remains one of the most successful and revered snappers in rock. He began his career as a photographer by sneaking a camera into rock concerts, taking photos of such established rock giants as Queen and Led Zeppelin before going professional working for the deceased mag *Circus*. He has photographed Aerosmith, Twisted Sister, Quiet Riot, Dio, Journey, Ozzy Osbourne and just about every other major rock and metal artist of the past 20 years. He has also photographed such celebrities as Drew Barrymore, Kim Basinger and Alec Baldwin. His photo for *Slippery When Wet* is one of the most recognized album sleeves in rock history. "After that album I got lots of gigs," he says.

TOM KEENLYSIDE AND LEMA MOON
Also credited were horn players Tom Keenlyside and Lema Moon. The former is a revered saxophonist and flautist who has worked with just about everyone, from Aerosmith to Tom Jones. As a Vancouver native, he didn't have far to travel for this job.

Lema Moon, however, is a pseudonym for none other than David Bryan, who is a very talented multi-instrumentalist in his own right. He has even co-written a musical called *Memphis*. It is probably fair to say that Richie Sambora has gathered most of the musical plaudits, partly because he is a great player, but also because guitarists are a far more visible breed on stage than keyboard players (with due deference to showman keyboardists such as Keith Emerson who manages to stick knives in his organ – ouch! – amongst other acts of cruelty to dumb keyboards, as well as brilliant playing) stuck away behind banks of keys. Make no mistake though, Bryan has been crucial in the development of the Bon Jovi sound and probably hasn't really got the credit he deserves because he isn't flashy, just tasteful and extremely good at what he does.

JBJ painted an affectionate picture of his early years with Bryan to Glenn O'Brien of SPIN magazine in April 1987: "I played in a couple of bands on and off. And he was going to college when I put the band together. He's Mr. Schmaltz. He played cocktail piano in a place called the Pink Elephant, playing stuff like 'Feelings'. His father made him play there."

David Bryan, keyboard player extraordinaire.
(*Ron Akiyama / Frank White Photo Agency*)

New Jersey's one and only Southside Johnny.
A great influence on Jon. (*Miho*)

PART THREE
LIFE AFTER
SLIPPERY WHEN WET

(David Scott)

10
NEW JERSEY –
THE ALBUM THAT FOLLOWED

So that's the story of *Slippery When Wet*, but what happened afterwards? How the heck do you follow something like that? For a lot of bands, trying to live up to the legacy of a mega-successful album is a real problem. No doubt Bon Jovi did their fair share of soul searching too, before deciding to revisit their roots with *New Jersey*. Perhaps after *Slippery When Wet* they thought it wise to give a statement of who they were and where they had come from. Maybe this helped to keep them grounded.

The US state of New Jersey has provided Bon Jovi with lots of inspiration throughout their entire career thus far. Perhaps the Garden State's most famous son is Bruce Springsteen, who has been a great influence on Jon Bon Jovi. However, as JBJ reminded us in an interview with Simon Witter of the *NME* in December 1988: "A lot of people do think of him when you say Jersey, and that's cool, but Southside Johnny's from Jersey too, and he was much more of an influence to me." Actually, everything in New Jersey seems interconnected. Southside Johnny was briefly in one of Springsteen's early bands, the wonderfully named Dr Zoom And The Sonic Boom. When Springsteen's former drummer Vini "Mad Dog" Lopez left the Lord Gunner Group, he was replaced by Tico Torres a few years before the latter joined Bon Jovi.

LET IT ROCK

Just to lay the Springsteen tag to rest, JBJ told Adrian Deevoy for *Q* magazine in January 1989 "I've never really wanted to be Bruce," he says sounding surprised, "I've always admired Bono. He has a great voice. And I've been a big fan of U2 since the *Boy* album."

It has been argued that there is a definable Jersey sound. It has a big Italian influence (which can be found in bands as diverse as Springsteen's E-Street Band and Frankie Valli And The Four Seasons) and a strong dance element with roots in soul and R&B. Springsteen himself was influenced by Van Morrison, for example. Lyrically, the concerns are real life situations. Bon Jovi are heirs to this tradition, which they have (consciously or not) made their own. Certainly they have the R&B, danceable music and they stand up for the blue collar people of America.

Of course, Bon Jovi have named an album after their native State and one of their most famous songs, "Livin' On A Prayer", is reflective of an aspect of life in NJ. Bon Jovi, like Springsteen, have remained home birds unlike a lot of bands who, when they make it big, move to New York or LA. Fellow New Jersey native, Joe Lynn Turner, formerly of Deep Purple and Rainbow says, "They [Bon Jovi] are pretty honest and forthcoming ... not a lot of phoniness. You know the saying, 'Ya gotta problem with that?' Along with the rest of the attitude: it's all Jersey, you don't find it anywhere else really ... It's the way people in Jersey are."

JBJ summed up his feelings about his home state to Simon Witter of the *NME* in 1988: "It's the same kind of attitude that places like Liverpool and Sheffield have, and places like London, New York, LA and Tokyo don't have. The small town, small state, underdog thing always kept you fighting, kept you looking up."

However, JBJ confessed to John Carccui at the *Huffington Post* in 2012 when asked about his status as a Jersey rocker: "Depends what day of the week that it is. Those are my roots. That truth helped us not fall into the trap of our peer group in the mid-'80s. Being from New Jersey was actually a great asset, now that I'm a much older, wiser man ... If you were to ask me about a mistake I have made, it's calling my fourth album *New Jersey*, because, for the first time in my life, we were compared to the E Street Band."

NEW JERSEY – THE ALBUM THAT FOLLOWED

The *Slippery When Wet* Tour was exhausting, but it was time to make a new album; by Christmas 1987 they already had demos of over 30 original songs for their new offering. They hooked up with songwriter Desmond Child and producer Bruce Fairbairn again at Little Mountain Sound Studios in Vancouver from 1 May-31 July 1988. There was certainly a lot going on behind the scenes: JBJ and Sambora founded the New Jersey Underground Music Company and their manager Doc McGhee had been in court, fighting charges of drug smuggling into the United States earlier in his life. He was subsequently found guilty of smuggling marijuana, but got away with a suspended sentence and fine, partly due to JBJ writing a six page letter to the judge asking for leniency, as a man in McGhee's position could do much good (and, fair play, he did organize a festival in the Soviet Union against drugs in that country and for world peace).

However, the show - or rather the album - had to go on. The bulk of the songwriting was done by Jon, Sambora and Child, although the trio wrote "Wild Is The Wind" with prolific hit writer Diane Warren and "Stick to Your Guns" was written by Jon, Sambora and Holly Knight. In fact, the band had written so many songs that they wanted the album to be a double release but the record company baulked at such an idea, thinking the fans could not afford the extra cost, which is often the response from a label. The extra tracks that were considered were: "Love Is War", "Let's Make It Baby", "The Boys Are Back In Town", "Outlaws Of Love", "Judgment Day", "Growing Up The Hard Way", "Does Anybody Really Fall In Love Anymore?", "Rosie", "River Of Love (Come Alive)", "Backdoor To Heaven", "Love Hurts", "Diamond Ring", "Now And Forever" and "Seven Days".

In terms of the album title, some names had been thrown around (one of them being the excellent *Sons Of Beaches* and another, apparently, the risqué *68 And I Owe You One*) but in the end they named it after the whole of their home state rather than just the Jersey Shore. This is something Jon at least would regret because it meant people would associate them with Bruce Springsteen. *New Jersey* was given a special promotional conference/listening session on 18 August 1988 at the Roseland Ballroom in New York. It was broadcast live by satellite to eleven US cities.

New Jersey was released in the US on 19 September 1988, reaching Number 1 and in the UK on 1 October 1988 where it also hit top spot, spending 47 weeks in the charts. It was their first British Number 1 album while in the States it was their second. To promote the album they committed themselves to 232 gigs during the next two years. The album spawned five global hit singles: "Bad Medicine", "Born To Be My Baby", "I'll Be There For You", "Lay Your Hands On Me" and "Living In Sin".

Chris Welch reviewed the album in *Metal Hammer*: "*New Jersey* is beautifully crafted which shows that for everything from charisma to engineering to sheer musicianship, Bon Jovi are way out in front."

At the time, the album quickly sold in its millions with a reputed seven million in the States alone and eighteen million worldwide. The album also picked up a fanbase in the former Soviet Union after it was released via the home grown Melodiya record label. The latest remastered version of the album comes with an enhanced CD video of "Lay Your Hands On Me".

New Jersey is a fine follow up to *Slippery When Wet*. The production, as you'd expect from the late great Bruce Fairbairn, is spot on. Whereas *SWW* album was consistent, *New Jersey* is more varied with a couple too many ballads, but some of the rock songs are certainly memorable: "Lay Your Hands On Me" and "Bad Medicine" are great songs to start an album of this kind. Bon Jovi had finally found their sound: good guitars, infectious melodies, harmonic backing vocals and a piano/keys intro. However, it was around this time that they started to become known as a "chicks' band" primarily because of their looks and surely this had an effect on their music? There are some good ballads here but also overly-sentimental ones such as "Wild Is The Wind". Also, "Ride Cowboy Ride" is just filler material. In the end, this is a fairly strong melodic rock album that leans a little too much toward the pop side but that doesn't stop it from being a really entertaining release.

NEW JERSEY – THE ALBUM THAT FOLLOWED

To promote their *New Jersey* album, which also gained top spot in Canada, Australia, New Zealand, Sweden, Russian, Brazil, Mexico, Japan and some European territories, Bon Jovi hit the road for their biggest and most exhaustive world tour, notching up 232 live dates beginning on 30 October 1988 and finishing on 17 February 1990. The last shows in Mexico have become famous. A student riot broke out on the very last night of the tour and delayed the band's performance. There is even video footage of it.

There is a funny story about the gig at the NEC in Birmingham, England where support was supposed to be by ex-Runaway Lita Ford, but she was unfortunately unwell that night. Enter the cavalry, in the shape of British melodic rock band Shy. Tony Mills, Shy's singer, remembers: "The show was packed with 11,000 people in the auditorium and the stage was magnificent. State of the art monitoring built beneath the stage, which was constructed of enormous aluminium grills was one of the most hi-tech set-ups that I ever walked across. I spoke to Jon briefly backstage to wish him a great show, but he was preoccupied as we all are before performances of such magnitude and due to other commitments I never got the chance to see him again ..."

Shy's Roy Davis explains, "Doc McGhee knew our manager and asked him if there were any local bands who could step in. Hence we got the call. What was hilarious though was that it very nearly didn't happen. I had gone to a local garden centre with the missus and had had a blazing row. Luckily enough, as it happens, this was in the days before mobile phones, because of the row we had gone home early and there had been a note stuck through the letter box saying I had to get to the NEC to support Bon Jovi ... I thought it was a wind up and threw the note in the bin. Then the phone calls started ... I still thought it was a wind up and because of the extremely bad mood, told everyone to fuck off! Eventually I got the message from the NEC that the crew were already there. Now I believed!"

Speaking about their 40 minute set, Davis says, "An awesome night, of course. Bon Jovi did their soundcheck and then there was an almighty bomb scare (still in the days of the IRA Troubles etc.,) so the building

Backstage pass from the homecoming gig at the Giants Stadium, NJ

had to be evacuated. So there we were outside the backstage area, all crews, all bands, drivers, everyone. Turns out, if I remember correctly ... The Pogues had played the night before and it was something to do with that ... The guys [Bon Jovi] were great. They came into the dressing room and introduced themselves to us. They were really cool and friendly. Unfortunately, because of the bomb scare, time was really short and we didn't have too long to chat."

So, what about Bon Jovi's crew and the local Birmingham audience? How did they react to Shy? Davis remembers, "The crew were fine. We actually knew quite a lot of the crew anyway, it was only the 'personals' that we didn't know and because we were of a 'certain level' at the time, we were given a certain amount of respect ... The audience were great. Because of the delay, due to the bomb scare, we had no chance for a soundcheck, etc. We literally wheeled the gear on stage and played! It was really funny because obviously no one knew that we were playing, but because it was Bon Jovi, most of our friends and family were in the audience anyway! To say they were shocked to see us is an understatement, but we certainly had our 'five mins of fame' in Birmingham."

The tour ran for ten legs and they were so busy that they had to film live footage for the music videos to "Lay Your Hands On Me", "I'll Be There For You" and "Blood On Blood". These can be viewed on the VHS releases *New Jersey: The Videos* and *Access All Areas*. Running for 45 minutes and released in 1989, *New Jersey: The Videos* features all the music videos from the album and has since been deleted. The single VHS release also featured interviews and backstage footage. But even better was the double VHS version (released in 1990) which featured the acclaimed behind the scenes documentary *Access All Areas: A Rock & Roll Odyssey*. Fans are eager to see a DVD version of this compilation. Dave Shack reviewed the collection in *Metal Forces*: "All in all a great stocking filler that might tide you over until the next album."

To illustrate the sheer size of the tour's production, Elianne Halbersberg wrote in *Kerrang!*: "... a massive sound system to drill every note right through your eardrums, pyro blasts, and a cable-suspended 'catwalk' that encircles the arena floor and allows our man of the hour [Jon] and his right-hand man, Richie Sambora, to (GASP!) run around the hall right over our very heads!"

During the New Jersey Syndicate Tour, which hit Europe, Japan, North America, Russia, Australia and New Zealand and South America, Billy Squier (along with Skid Row) supported Bon Jovi at the Giants Stadium, New Jersey in a gig dubbed "The Homecoming" on 11 June. It was apt as Bon Jovi are Giants fans.

Squier: "In 1989, Bon Jovi was on top of the world. Jon rang me up and asked me if I wanted to do a string of dates to kick off his New Jersey Syndicate Tour. This made sense, as I'd been off the road and out of the public eye for a few years, and as the saying goes, 'Out of sight, out of mind.' I had a new record coming out and the timing seemed perfect. Only hitch was, Jon was offering me a paltry sum of money to do most of the shows. He reasoned that my playing with him would resuscitate my career and therefore, I should be happy to do the dates regardless of the lack of financial consideration. He said that if I wasn't interested, he'd give the dates to Bad English, who'd be happy to have them. We ultimately settled on one gig at Giants Stadium, at terms we both agreed upon."

On 12 and 13 August they performed at the Moscow Music Peace Festival alongside Mötley Crüe, Ozzy Osbourne, Skid Row, Cinderella and the Scorpions. This was organized by Doc McGhee and was part of the rehabilitation after his drugs bust. Photographer Mark Weiss recalls: "I was on the plane with them; I was their official photographer. I think that Doc was managing Bon Jovi and Mötley Crüe. No one was really big in Russia; it was just all hype from America, so anyone could have been the headliner and they would have believed them. I guess the biggest two bands that were there was Bon Jovi and Mötley Crüe. It was supposed to be an equal billing kind of thing so Mötley went on first; Bon Jovi went on … and I think the story was that no one was supposed to get pyro or do anything special or whatever. Jon's running down the aisle with a Russian outfit on, a jacket and a hat, and going down the aisle from the soundboard to the stage with all the guards parting the fans in the way of everything. I think he had some pyro and all that … I think maybe Tommy [Lee] got mad at Doc. Someone punched someone. I don't know who."

From Moscow, the band flew to England to perform at the iconic Monsters Of Rock festival at the Milton Keynes National Bowl on 19 August. In fact, having been on the road since '84, Jon had persistent voice problems and had to hire a vocal coach; he vowed to pace himself after the tour climaxed in 1990. The New Jersey Syndicate Tour was also fraught with internal squabbling, health issues and personal problems.

Despite all that, they managed to put their personal differences aside for some benefit shows at the end of 1990; Doc McGhee was integral in getting the band together and acting as peacemaker.

The good that came out of the tour was that Bon Jovi had become one of the world's biggest touring acts, they had two massive selling albums under their belt and, for future reference, they knew how to handle a busy touring schedule without experiencing the same problems they had encountered from '88 to '90.

What a great team. Jon and Richie at Madison Square Garden August 1987.
(John T Comerford 111 / Frank White Photo Agency)

11
FROM MELODIC HARD ROCK TO POP ROCK – BON JOVI IN THE PRESENT DAY

It was obvious Bon Jovi wanted to be taken more seriously and to do that some changes had to be made. At least on the surface, to fans that adored those first four albums, that's how it seemed.

They followed the duo of *Slippery When Wet* and *New Jersey* with 1992's *Keep The Faith*, however, during the interim the band members went on to make solo albums after the truly tiring New Jersey Syndicate Tour which basically burnt them out. *Keep The Faith*, their fifth album, was a totally different sounding album from any of their previous full length studio releases. Grunge offered mighty opposition to the poodle-haired rock stars of the 1980s and during this period Bon Jovi sported a new look with fashionable clothes and haircuts to match.

They recorded *Keep The Faith* with producer Bob Rock who had been promoted from sound engineer on the band's previous two albums, *Slippery When Wet* and *New Jersey*. Recording took place at Little Mountain Sound Studios between December 1991 and August 1992. Mixing was done by Randy Straub and the engineering was done by Straub and Rock. Speaking to Malcolm Dome at *Metal Forces* in 1993, Jon said: "This is a Bon Jovi record for the '90s. You know, I can never repeat old formulae. There is no point in going backwards, that's just bullshit … I made this record for myself." The album was a hit and peaked at Number 5 on the *Billboard* 200, while it hit Number 1 in the UK. The band also went on a very successful promotional world tour and appeared on *MTV Unplugged* in 1992. The new album certainly represented a new phase in the band's career; one which was diametrically opposed to the *Slippery When Wet* era. Consequently, they lost some fans but gained some new ones along the way too. Reviewing *Keep The Faith* in *Kerrang!* (October, 1992) Paul Elliott had some scathing comments: "These days, when Bon Jovi play straightforward hard rock, it's without passion or conviction." But he ended his mixed review by saying, "… *Keep The Faith* has something for everyone; rock, ballads, pop, whatever."

To celebrate this new phase in their career the band released a compilation of greatest hits titled *Cross Road* which was released in October 1994 and went on to sell over three million copies worldwide. It topped the charts in many countries, including the US. At best, *Cross Road* is a predictable collection of songs. All the ones you'd expect to be here are here but, as it's a "best of" rather than a "greatest hits", the band could have used some imagination and handpicked some obscure gems to spice things up. After winning the "Best Selling Rock Band" award at the World Music Awards in 1994, bassist Alec John Such left the band and was replaced - albeit on an unofficial basis - by Hugh McDonald. McDonald was no stranger to the band, having played bass on "Runaway".

In June 1995, Bon Jovi unleashed their sixth studio album, *These Days*, which continued their more mature, albeit less rock orientated, sound. While *Slippery When Wet* and *New Jersey* can be seen as a pair, so can *Keep The Faith* and *These Days*. It has been said many times that *These Days* is Bon Jovi's darkest album; many of the issues written about in the lyrics include depression, despair, homelessness and poverty. Just listen to JBJ scream out the chorus during "Hey God" - perhaps he has never sounded so convincing. Bon Jovi had gone for a different style of music on *Keep The Faith* but this album goes one step deeper. The album was another hit, hitting Number 1 in the UK and various international markets, showing yet again that perhaps the band's fanbase was stronger outside of their native USA. The band continued to pick up more awards, including "Best International Band" at the BRIT Awards and "Best Rock Band" at the MTV European Music Awards. *These Days* saw the band commit to yet another world tour; one which broke records at London's Wembley Stadium when the band played three sold out nights in June 1995.

How could the band top the success of *These Days*? Well, mirroring their decision to take a break after the overwhelming success of *New Jersey*, the band took another lengthy break to work on various solo projects. They regrouped in 1999 for the album *Crush*, which saw the band go back to a more rock-orientated sound. While many of Bon Jovi's 1980s *Kerrang!*-reading hardened rock enthusiasts had lost touch with the band, they still had a huge fanbase, with a higher proportion of female fans than most other rock bands. To prove that Bon Jovi's new album harked back to the past, "It's My Life" references Jon's fictional characters Tommy and Gina who were made famous in "Livin' On A Prayer". "It's My Life" was a hit single and one which stands up with some of their most famous songs and has since become a firm live favourite.

The awards continued to fill the band's mantelpiece and they played to thousands of fans around the world during 2000, which included two stops at Wembley Stadium. Touring continued into 2001, which also included two sold out homecoming gigs at the Giants Stadium. It certainly seemed as though the band had done much to redefine their sound and image and leave their 1980s albums firmly in the past, although it was obvious that fans craved songs from *Slippery When Wet* and *New Jersey* more vehemently than any of their new material, regardless of how successful the new material might be.

In 2001, they celebrated their success as a live band by releasing their first ever live album, *One Wild Night Live 1985–2001*. The album includes songs taken from the band's archives and as such lacks the thrills of a single live performance, but it sold well, of course. They won the "Hottest Live Show" award at the 2001 MY VH-1 Music Awards.

Moving into 2002, the band regrouped for their eighth full length studio album and one which reflected the feelings of angst and the emotions felt

Jon and Richie onstage in Dublin, 2006.
(*James Anderson*)

across the country after 9/11. *Bounce* saw the band produce their heaviest rock album since *New Jersey*; one which houses distorted guitars, fairly heavy riffs (for Bon Jovi) and more rock-sounding vocals. Fans inevitably warmed to the album; some more than others but the band continued to have their fair share of critics with lots of pundits arguing that Bon Jovi's music follows a preconceived formula. Ian Fortnam gave the album 3/5 in *Classic Rock* magazine and said: "... pretty much business as usual. Slick production jobs; chocolate box sentiments; the odd smidgen of rock cliché ..." The band launched yet another hugely successful world tour in support of their new record.

LET IT ROCK

The band re-worked some of their classic songs for *This Left Feels Right* in 2002. They rewrote and re-recorded twelve of their biggest hits, including "Wanted Dead Or Alive", "Livin' On A Prayer" and "You Give Love A Bad Name" from *Slippery When Wet*. The album inevitably received mixed feedback from fans and many critics asked the question: What is the point?

In 2004, the band released the archive box set *100,000,000 Bon Jovi Fans Can't Be Wrong*, the title of which is a pun on the Elvis Presley box set *50,000,000 Elvis Fans Can't Be Wrong*. The Jovi box set is certainly of interest to fans of Bon Jovi's 1980s work.

The band were now feeling a thirst to return to the studio with some new material in hand and so they released their ninth album, *Have A Nice Day*, in 2005, and debates began to arise with rock fans about whether Bon Jovi can accurately be labelled a rock band anymore, given their tendency towards the more commercial pop side of music. *Have A Nice Day* had been recorded at Jon's personal recording facility, Sanctuary II Studios in New Jersey, with additional recording being completed at Henson Studios in LA. It was produced by John Shanks, Jon and Sambora with Desmond Child as executive producer. Rick Parashar (producer of Alice In Chains and Pearl Jam) also co-produced some tracks with Jon and Sambora ("Wildflower", "Last Cigarette", "Novocaine" and "Story"); the idea was probably to give the album an even harder and more contemporary rock sound. It worked, to an extent. The album was a hit and it appeared that Bon Jovi were incapable of releasing a commercial flop given the sheer bulk of their global fanbase. The 2005 to 2006 world tour was not their most extensive in terms of dates, but it was certainly financially rewarding and one which saw the band play at some of the world's biggest stadiums.

In a shock-horror moment for rock fans and the final straw for a lot of long standing rockers, Bon Jovi released the country-flavoured album *Lost Highway* in 2007, which hit Number 1 in the USA and various international markets. Inspired by their collaboration with Jennifer Nettles of Sugarland on the country crossover track "Who Says You Can't Go Home", Bon Jovi had decided to make an album of Nashville influenced songs and it certainly worked on a commercial level. It seems that there comes a time in many a rocker's life when it is time to hit the dirt road to Nashville to make a country album, as Robert Plant will testify.

They also performed yet another mammoth trek, which saw the band perform at the London venue the 02 Arena (previously known as the Millennium Dome) in June 2007, making them the first band to perform there. It was one of the highest earning tours of 2007, grossing over $200 million.

To celebrate 25 years, the band released the documentary *When We Were Beautiful* in 2009 and then unleashed their new album, *The Circle*, in November. It was touted as a return to the band's earlier rock sound but some critics felt the album lacked originality. However, it hit Number 1 in the USA and the band began a world tour in February 2010, dubbed The Circle Tour. They stayed on the road well into 2011, by which point the tour morphed into Bon Jovi Live. The change in the tour's name was perhaps related to the release of the band's first *Greatest Hits* album, which had been released in November 2010. The album covers the period 1983 to 2010 and includes various songs from *Slippery When Wet*, namely the obvious choices: "Livin' On A Prayer", "You Give Love A Bad Name" and "Wanted Dead Or Alive".

Bon Jovi remains a hugely popular live band in the 21st century, despite the often less than stellar quality of their studio work in recent years. Kas Mercer of Mercenary PR remembers: "Once at the Milton Keynes Bowl, they had a bar on stage and the label ran a competition so fans could go behind the bar and serve the band drinks as they played. I had to look after the comp winners, so I was on stage for over half the set. Another one was when they busked in Covent Garden; we weren't allowed to let anyone know until an hour before, but it was still mobbed. It was funny watching the reactions of people just passing by when they realized it really WAS Bon Jovi."

LET IT ROCK

Mónica Castedo-López of *Fireworks: The Melodic Rock Magazine* recalls:

I started listening to rock music when I was about 12; and one of the first bands that caught my eye and my ear due to the ample mass media coverage was Bon Jovi. Their music was fresh, powerful, rocking and moving. I would take the big cassette player that my grandad bought me to the park and listen to their tapes over and over again with some friends. This was the time of the *Slippery When Wet* album. Years went by and when I was 22, in 1996, they announced a gig in El Molinón football stadium in Gijón, Spain. By then I was a bit more affluent and I could afford the trip; I drove four odd hours with some friends, and my boyfriend at the time, to see the gig. This was one of the first big shows I'd ever been to and the expectations were high even though I wasn't sure what to expect. When I walked in, I remember I was shocked by the high proportion of women – or girls, rather – compared to men. Girls were chanting the band's name, cheering hysterically and almost fainting when the band turned up onstage. I had only read about this sort of behaviour in magazines or seen it on TV, but my naive brain never wanted to accept it as reality that women could behave in such a manner.

It's been many years since that show and my memory is not the greatest of them all, but this is one of the two main facts that I remember of that 4 June gig. The other was my amazement at seeing the band immaculately perform anthems such as "Keep The Faith", "You Give Love A Bad Name" and "Bad Medicine". I was awed by the charisma and self-confidence of each member, particularly of Richie Sambora and Jon. How could just five guys draw the attention of such a big crowd and keep it going for the two hours that the show lasted? That was genius ... Great musicians, fantastic performance and an awesome show. May they continue for many more years.

In November 2012 the band released a digital-only video called *Inside Out* which consists of shows recorded at the O2 Arena, MetLife Stadium and Madison Square Garden. The work was released via cinemas before it was available to stream on iTunes.

Moving into 2013, the band released their brand new studio album *What About Now* in March, which was recorded before Sambora's third solo effort, *Aftermath Of The Lowdown*, released in September 2012. To coincide with their new album the band launched the mammoth world trek Because We Can – The Tour, which consisted of trips around North America, Europe, Africa, Far East, Australia and South America.

Speaking about the album-tour-album cycle, JBJ spoke to the *Huffington Post*'s John Carucci in 2012: "I know how to do it. It's as simple as that ... New songs are why artists go on the road. That's why I go on the road. It's a three-prong play. Writing: You're intrigued. Recording: It brings it to life. And then you want to share it."

However, the touring got a bit much for Richie Sambora, who quit the Because We Can Tour citing he was missing his daughter growing up. He told the *Hollywood Reporter*: "You're talking 24/7, and you don't get to come home. I missed so much of my child's life. And you get to that place where you realize, 'Oh, my god, this is really important.'" To cap it all, his mother wasn't well either, so it is understandable. His place on the tour was taken by Canadian axeman Phil X Xenedis. Sambora claims that he hopes to rejoin the band sometime. Let's hope so.

This tour was generally problematical for the band as Tico Torres was briefly hospitalized with a gall bladder problem and replaced by Rich Scannella.

Meantime, rock royalty Jon Bon Jovi was rubbing shoulders with real royalty in the shape of Prince William, the Queen of England's grandson. At a charity event in London in November 2013, JBJ, William and Taylor Swift belted out a version of "Livin' On A Prayer". It is unlikely that Prince William will join the band, having other commitments!

Guitarist Bruce Kulick, who was in KISS when Bon Jovi supported them in late 1984, says, "I am very impressed with the continued massive success, and they deserve it for sure ... Recently I did a favour for a friend who needed some talk box guitar stuff like 'Livin' On A Prayer,' so that was a trip. And in retrospect there was a song I did with Eric Carr that wound up on his *Rockology* CD that was strongly reminiscent of the band. So they definitely have been an influence for me."

Let's leave the last word in this section to the man that signed Bon Jovi, Derek Shulman:

LET IT ROCK

Bon Jovi the band and Jon Bon Jovi the man have withstood the tests of time and musical shifts and fads for over 25 years in a business that spits out stars that shine and fizzle in a space of a year these days. This band is the essence of what artists and their representatives should and can be for the future. Develop your skills and your chops over a period of time. Become great performers live, write GREAT songs and believe in yourself whether the record company is there or not. Jon Bon Jovi did and still does 25 years later.

Enough said!

12
BACKSTAGE AREA – THOUGHTS & REMINISCENCES ON BON JOVI

I invited the following musicians, and others, backstage to talk about Bon Jovi and their impact on the rock world …

Steve Blaze (Lillian Axe): "I met Jon once when Lillian Axe played Houston, right when his first album came out. I hung out with the first bassist [Alec John Such] at a guitar show in Florida when I was there as a featured artist … I highly respect the band and what they have accomplished. They have mastered the art of writing songs that appeal to a large cross section of the public. Very talented group. Their music is honest and passionate."

Ron Boudreau (Photographer): "I was Skid Row photographer on tour with Skid Row/Bon Jovi in the summer of 1989. Jon showed up at a Skid Row autograph session in Toronto. When Jon came in through the back of the record store, I snapped my first photo of him. Later that night after the concert, Skid Row was doing a second show at Sebastian's [Bach, Skid

(David Scott)

Row's singer] fav Toronto rock club Rock 'n' Roll Heaven. Towards the end of the Skid Row set, Jon jumped up on stage with the band and I was able to grab a few great shots of Jon and Sebastian!"

Dokken (Dokken): "I knew Jon back in the day when he was just starting out; we hung out at [Ratt drummer] Bobby Blotzer's after their show with Ratt at The Forum in LA. It was the glory days for most of us then, then the '90s came and everything changed, I thought the first band that would take a hit was Bon Jovi, but they went to Europe and broke out there, which I thought would be impossible because they're too pop for the Europeans. But they did it and came back to the States stronger than ever. We toured with them in about '95 and their fans didn't care less about us even though we have sold millions as well. It was an eye opener! After the first show Richie says to me, 'It's a whole new world of fans out there.' Of all the bands from our era, Bon Jovi have survived through all the music changes the best, and I give them a high-five for that. They're still a great band: tight, professional and still nice guys. That's hard to be when you're one of the biggest bands on the planet …"

Robert Fleischman (Former Journey singer): "Bon Jovi ... a perfect example of timing: MTV was starting out and they had a great rock video and image; a chick magnet lead singer and the songs to back it all up, and to do that you have to have a great work ethic, to achieve what they've done. And they have done it for quite some years. Hats off to Bon Jovi!"

Tony Franklin (Bassist): "Blue Murder opened for them for about ten days in mid-1989. We didn't see too much of the band, though we hung a bit. JBJ is just a few days older than me ... a fellow Aries. They treated us well, good guys."

Holly Knight (Musician/songwriter): "I saw Bon Jovi live at Irvine [California.] I flew there in a helicopter with Don Johnson, who was the 'Man Of The Moment' on *Miami Vice*. I remember it was kind of surrealistic for me; I brought Don backstage to meet Jon and there I was, sandwiched in between the two of them, wearing this tight long black dress, and they're both commenting on how they loved working with me! And all I could think is: this [song]writing gig is cool! Who would've thought Beethoven could lead to moments like this. Pretty crazy ..."

Bruce Kulick (Former KISS guitarist): "We enjoyed Bon Jovi, but at the time I think they were still finding their sound. So we referred to them as a New Jersey band ... working hard to get to the top in other words. We knew that Jon was a star and that the band had huge potential. I remember meeting Jon at a club in the UK and he was so proud to have press on him in *Kerrang!* etc. He seemed to be genuine and ambitious."

Jason McMaster (Dangerous Toys): "The day that we shot the back cover of the first Dangerous Toys release (somewhere around November/December, 1988) Bon Jovi - with a new band called Skid Row - were playing in Austin, Texas where I live. The photographer was the infamous Mark Weiss who is also from New Jersey, where Jovi as well as Skid Row are from; they just happened to all be friends. Mark got all of us into the show, backstage and the like ... We did photos with Skid Row, and Jon Bon Jovi was kind enough to take a quick candid shot with yours truly and the only known print of that was in an issue of *Metal Edge* magazine (USA) during that summer of 1989. He was very nice, but I gotta say, even though I am not a fan of his music; he is a great songwriter and all his band mates were super cool to us ..."

Billy Squier (Singer-songwriter): "I first met Jon when he was more than likely still 'John'. This would have been late '70s, when he was in a band from Tom's River called The Rest. Jack Ponti, the lead guitarist, came to me and asked if I'd help them out with some demos. Jon hadn't found himself at this point – heck, he was barely street-legal, and the days of big hair and MTV were still a ways off. But he knew where he wanted to be ... and this is what stuck in my mind: HE KNEW WHERE HE WANTED TO BE ... and was prepared to do whatever it took to get there. Having talent is one thing – having the perseverance to stick it out when talent doesn't get you through is a whole other trip. Jon took that trip ... which is why he's where he is today."

Marc Storace (Krokus): "I once shook hands and exchanged greetings with Jon Bon Jovi at the celebrity launching party for the then brand new US magazine SPIN in New York City, somewhere back in the mid-'80s. It was a meet and greet event for the US Press, where I also remember meeting the late great John Entwistle, bass player of The Who. Bon Jovi had the hit single 'Runaway' in the charts shortly before that."

Mike Tramp (White Lion): "I have been lucky enough to have been on stage with Jon and the band twice. Once was on my birthday in 1989, when Bon Jovi played in Hawaii. Jon invited me up to sing with him and we performed Thin Lizzy's 'The Boys Are Back In Town'. The second time was in San Diego and I joined him again for Free's 'All Right Now'."

Joe Lynn Turner (Former Deep Purple & Rainbow singer): "Yeah, they are a great rock band and still going strong. It was very different in our hair band days. It was less corporate, more gritty rock and roll as far as the scene goes. Desmond Child and I even wrote a song with him [called] 'Rage Of Angels' which was vowed not to be released and that's too bad. Desmond did take the middle section and put it into … [an] Aerosmith song so he obviously used it later; it was also very reminiscent of 'Livin' On A Prayer' but that is only natural and it happens when people collaborate."

Jonathan Valen (Former Legs Diamond drummer): "When I was on the Andy Taylor tour we were playing at the NHK Hall in Tokyo, Japan. After our show, we decided to go to a club called the Lexington Queen in Roppongi; our guitar player, Paul Hansen, brought an amp and a guitar and was playing his mayhem to everyone in the club. And much to my surprise there was Tico Torres, sitting in the back of the club with a few girls having a drink. We spent the whole night rallying with him … lots of fun!"

Mark Weiss (Photographer): "I went to South America with them for six weeks in the '90s. I videotaped that whole tour … All the roadies and everyone went on the plane. It was crazy. It was like Elvis; it was really nuts. No rules, no one had their seat belts on. I shot all their weddings. I shot Jon's kids' Christenings."

Greg Wells (Producer): "He [Jon] was totally cool. Very professional, focussed, generous, and wanted the best results out of everything and everyone including himself."

Ron Wikso (Drummer): "Sure, I've seen them live several times. I think they sound way better with Hugh [McDonald] than they ever did with Alec [John Such] but of course, I'm sure they'd tell you that too. I also think they're a pretty consistently good sounding band. I've always thought that Richie was a better singer than Jon but Jon is certainly a great front man

LET IT ROCK

and showman. Tico is a solid drummer, who I think sounds better with Hugh, and David has always done a great job on keyboards. Of course, Richie sounds great on guitar and he and Jon singing together always sounds good. They've always had great production too ... video screens etc. It's usually a pretty entertaining night going to a Bon Jovi show."

One thing that comes out of this book is what a great guy Richie Sambora is. He has been as important to the band as JBJ and a creative force of nature in his own right. So, to ensure he gets his share of the limelight, I invited some folks to talk about Sambora. Let's hope he returns to his rightful place in the band.

Tommy Mandel (Keyboardist): "Richie was one of the nicest, most musical, generous guys I ever worked for. And I hear he's one of the world's great lovers, although I don't know that from personal experience. He loves all kinds of music, and you can listen to him tell stories of meeting the great and the strange of our planet, for hours. He could do stand up if he weren't such a musical force. Playing in his band was a trip. His best buddy, David Bryan, had hurt his hand before the tour, so Kasim Sulton reminded Richie of me, (since we'd done a bit of work together on Bon Jovi's second album, mostly programming ...) and the next thing I knew, I was flying out to LA (from NYC) to rehearse. It was a pleasure, almost like a perpetual jam session with the best cats: Everett Bradley and Gioia Bruno on percussion and vocals, Kasim, Richie, Ron Wikso, and Richie Supa – the songs were pretty deep, so we just played them with respect, and Richie did his soulful thing out front.

After playing in Bryan Adams' band for so many years, I appreciated the free interplay between the musicians, or maybe it was just the change. Bryan's band was smaller, and playing with Bryan is an insane amount of fun too, but going into Richie's band was like putting on a different pair of shoes after ten years in one pair, even if it was the best ones you could imagine – the change was fun. Plus the styles: sort of like going from AC/DC into Steely Dan. But better of course! Ha. And the guy whose parts I was recreating was Bill Preston! It was an education too."

Tom Marolda (Songwriter/musician): "When Richie is in work mode, he's unstoppable and very creative. This song ['One Light Burning'] was pouring out of the both of us at the time. I was pleased to see it hit the charts as well, but I'm not sure who put the brakes on its upward climb. That may have been the demise of Bon Jovi had it become a huge hit. Writing other songs with Richie took place at his Westlake home when he was married to Heather. I lived down the street from him and had a small home studio where we could demo new material. Working with Richie, as I said, was very exciting when he was in his creative mode, but as the pressures of stardom and his personal life took a toll on him, I found Richie's creative output suffering and putting a strain on our relationship. I have only fond and warm memories of my friend as he stood in my corner for many years. I just hope that he can put his life on the right track and continue his amazing journey."

Stuart Smith (Guitarist): "I've always loved Richie's voice as much as his guitar playing, to my mind he's one of the most soulful singers there is. When I first got the record deal to do a solo album I put together a 'wish list' of who I'd like on it and Richie was one of my first calls. I said to Richie: 'Listen, I don't want you to do this just because you're my brother-in-law but I'd really like you to sing a track on my album' and he said: 'Great, no one ever asks me to sing' so I sent him the tracks of 'When A Blind Man Cries' and 'Do You Ever Think Of Me'. When Richie turned up at the studio he had his guitars with him and when I asked why he'd brought them he said he liked the tracks so much he'd like to play on them, which was just fine by me. He sang 'When A Blind Man Cries' first and did an amazing job ... I've always felt that if Richie went out on his own he'd be our next Clapton."

Kasim Sultan (Utopia/The New Cars): "I've known Richie and Jon for some years now and have a tremendous amount of respect for their talent and success. In 1998, I was attending the NAMM Trade Show in Los Angeles and happened to run into Richie. He had just finished his second solo record and was preparing to put some dates together for a tour. I mentioned that I had some time off and if he needed a bass player, I would jump at the chance to work with him. A few phone calls later I found myself in rehearsals for what would turn out to be a year on and off the road with his band visiting Australia, Japan, the UK and Germany. I can't remember having a better time with any artist I've ever worked with. Not only is Richie one of the best guitarists in music today, I can't say I've ever been treated better by anyone in the business before or since. His kindness and respect for me touched me so deeply that I felt compelled to write his mother a letter telling her what a wonderful person her son is."

Ron Wikso (Drummer): "Richie's a great guy, a great singer, a great guitar player and he really treated the band incredibly well. I always thought, and I told him this, that he could have taken his solo career a lot further and become sort of the Clapton of his generation. He's got great charisma, he's a genuinely nice guy and he has a blast on the gigs, which shows through to the audience and is infectious when you're playing with him on stage. Of all the bands/tours I've been involved with, that was one of my favourites."

PART FOUR
TOUR DATES & DISCOGRAPHY

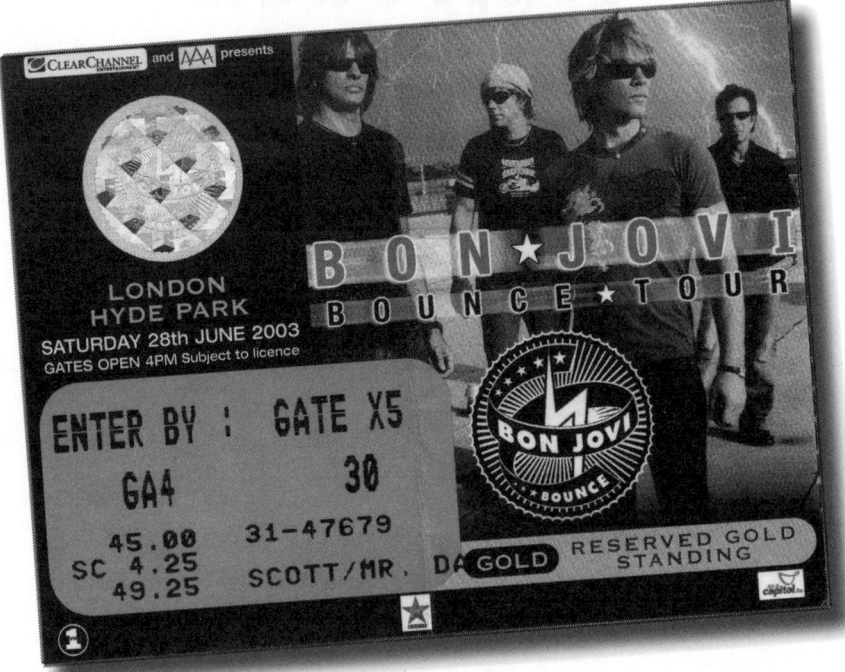

(David Scott)

THE *SLIPPERY WHEN WET* TOUR DATES 1986-1987

1986

CANADA
(Opening for Judas Priest on their Fuel For Life Tour on Canadian dates)
14 July: Pacific Coliseum, Vancouver
16 July: Olympic Saddledome, Calgary
17 July: Shaw Conference Centre, Edmonton
19 July: Winnipeg Arena
22 July: CNE Stadium, Toronto
23 July: Montreal Forum
24 July: Colisée de Quebec
25 July: Ottawa Civic Centre

JAPAN
11 August: Nagoya - Aichi Kosei Nenkinkaikan, Nagoya
12 August: Fukuoka - Fukuoka Sunplace
13 & 14 August: Osaka - Festival Hall
16 August: Kobe - Kobe International House
18 August: Tokyo - Nippon Budokan
20 August: Yokohama - Yokohama Cultural Gymnasium
21 August: Sendai - Miyagi Prefectural Auditorium
23 August: Aomori - Aomori Civic Cultural Hall
25 August: Sapporo - Hokkaido Koseinenkin Hall

USA
12 September: Meadowlands Arena, East Rutherford, NJ (opening for .38 Special)
13 September: Mansfield, Great Woods, MA (opening for .38 Special)
28 September: Pelham, Oak Mountain Amphitheatre, AL (opening for .38 Special)
7 October: Midsouth Coliseum, Memphis, TN (opening for .38 Special)
15 October: Capital Centre, Largo, MD (opening for Ratt)

EUROPE
(Queensrÿche and FM supported)
07 November: St George's Hall, Bradford
09 November: Ipswich Gaumont

LET IT ROCK

10 November: Sheffield City Hall
11 November: Birmingham Odeon
12 November: Edinburgh Playhouse
14 November: Manchester Apollo
15 November: Newcastle City Hall
17 & 18 November: London, Hammersmith Odeon
20 November: Liverpool Royal Court Theatre
21 November: Victoria Hall Stoke On Trent
23 November: Leicester, De Montfort Hall
24 & 25 November: London, Hammersmith Odeon
26 November: St George's Hall, Bradford
27 November: Rijnhal, Arnhem
28 November: Le Zenith, Paris
29 November: CIG De Malley, Lausanne
30 November: Carl-Diem-Halle Würzburg
02 December: Westfalenhallen, Dortmund
03 December: Eilenriedhalle, Hannover
04 December: K.B. Hallen, Copenhagen
06 December: Johanneshovs Isstadion, Stockholm
08 December: Helsinki Ice Hall

USA
(Cinderella supported)

19 December: Baltimore Arena, MD
20 December: Stabler Arena, Bethlehem, PA
21 December: Cambria County War Memorial Arena, Johnstown, PA
26 December: Cumberland County Civic Centre, Portland, ME
27 December: The Centrum, Worcester, MA
29 December: Baltimore Arena, MD
30 December: New Haven Coliseum, CT
31 December: Meadowlands Arena, East Rutherford, NJ

1987

USA

02 January: Hersheypark Arena, PA
03 January: Kingston Armory, Wilkes-Barre, PA
04 January: Utica Memorial Auditorium, NY
09 January: McNichols Arena, Denver, CO
10 January: Tingley Coliseum, Albuquerque, NM
11 January: County Coliseum, El Paso, TX
13 January: Tucson Convention Centre, AZ
14 January: Arizona Veterans Memorial Coliseum, Phoenix, AZ
16 January: San Diego Sports Arena, CA
17 January: Thomas & Mack Centre, Paradise, Las Vegas, NV
19 January: Orange Pavilion, San Bernardino, CA
20 January: Selland Arena, Fresno, CA
21 January: Long Beach Arena, CA
23 January: Lawlor Events Centre, Reno, NV
24 January: Cow Palace, Daly City, CA
26 January: Spokane Coliseum, WA
27 January: Center Coliseum, Seattle, WA
31 January: Coliseum, Tyler, TX
02 February: Reunion Arena, Dallas, TX
03 February: Memorial Coliseum, Corpus Christi, TX
04 February: Majestic Theatre, San Antonio, TX
06 February: Lake Charles Civic Centre, LA
07 February: The Summit, Houston, TX
08 February: Frank Erwin Center, Austin, TX
10 February: Hirsch Memorial Coliseum, Shreveport, LA
11 February: Humphrey Coliseum, Starkville, MS
12 February: Mississippi Coast Coliseum, Biloxi, MS
14 February: Hollywood Sportatorium, Pembroke Pines, FL
15 February: Bayfront Center, St. Petersburg, FL
17 February: Lee County Civic Centre, North Fort Myers, FL
18 February: Jacksonville Coliseum, FL

PUERTO RICO
February 20: San Juan - Roberto Clemente Coliseum
February 21: San Juan - Hiram Bithorn Stadium

USA
24 February: The Myriad, Oklahoma City, OK
26 February: Kemper Arena, Kansas City, KS
27 February: Kiel Auditorium, St. Louis, MO
28 February: Barton Coliseum, Little Rock, AR
01 March: Hirsch Memorial Coliseum, LA
02 March: Humphrey Coliseum, Starkville, MS
03 March: Market Square Arena, Indianapolis, IN
04 & 05 March: UIC Pavilion, Chicago, IL
06 March: Mayo Civic Arena, Rochester, MN
08 March: MECCA Arena, Milwaukee, WI
10 & 11 March: Cobo Arena, Detroit, MI
12 March: Market Square Arena, Indianapolis, IN
14 March: Rockford Metrocentre, IL

CANADA
15 March: Colisée Pepsi, Quebec City

USA
18 March: Cincinnati Gardens, OH
19 March: Freedom Hall Civic Center, Johnson City, TN
20 March: Rupp Arena, Lexington, KY
23 & 24 March: The Omni, Atlanta, GA
25 March: Charlotte Coliseum, NC
27 March: Pittsburgh Civic Arena, PA
28 March: Buffalo Memorial Auditorium, NY
30 March: Richfield Coliseum, OH
31 March: Huntington Civic Coliseum, WV
02 April: The Spectrum, Philadelphia, PA
03 April: Hartford Civic Centre, Hartford, CT
04 & 05 April: The Spectrum, Philadelphia, PA
07 & 08 April: Uniondale - Nassau Veterans Memorial Coliseum, Uniondale, NY
09 April: Broome County Veterans Memorial Arena, Binghamton, NY

THE *SLIPPERY WHEN WET* TOUR DATES 1986–1987

10 April: Houston Fieldhouse, Troy, NY
11 April: Springfield Civic Centre, MA
13 April: Coliseum, Largo, MD
15 & 16 April: The Spectrum, Philadelphia, PA
01 & 02 May: Providence Civic Centre, RI
03 May: Oanondaga War Memorial, Syracuse, NY
05 May: Pittsburgh Civic Arena, PA
06 May: Richfield Coliseum, OH
08 May: Richmond Coliseum, VA
09 May: Greensboro Coliseum, NC
10 May: Hampton Coliseum, VA
12 May: Von Braun Civic Centre, Huntsville, AL
13 May: James White Civic Coliseum, Knoxville, TN
14 May: Birmingham-Jefferson Convention Complex, Birmingham, AL
16 May: Starwood Amphitheatre, Nashville, TN
17 May: Iowa State Fair, Des Moines, IA
18 May: Kiel Auditorium, St. Louis, MO
19 May: Iowa State Fair, Des Moines, IA
20 May: War Memorial Coliseum, Fort Wayne, IN
21 May: Market Square Arena, Indianapolis, IN
22 May: Freedom Hall, Louisville, KY
23 May: Kellogg Arena, Battle Creek, MI
24 May: Buckeye Lake Music Centre, Thornville, OH
27, 28 & 29 May: Joe Louis Arena, Detroit, MI
31 May: Rosemont Horizon, Chicago, IL
5 June: Rockford Metrocentre, IL
6 & 7 June: Met Center, Minneapolis, MN
9 June: Peoria Civic Center, IL
10 June: Five Seasons Centre, Cedar Rapids, IA
11 June: Kansas City – Kemper Arena, Kansas City, KS
13 June: Casper Events Centre, WY
14 & 15: McNichols Sports Arena, Denver, CO
17 & 18 June: Salt Lake City – Salt Palace, Salt Lake City, UT
20, 21 & 22 June: Irvine Meadows Amphitheater, Irvine, CA
25, 26 & 27 June: Shoreline Amphitheatre, Mountain View, CA
29 & 30 June: Memorial Coliseum, Portland, OR

LET IT ROCK

CANADA
02 July: Pacific Coliseum, Vancouver

USA
03 July: Rubber Bowl, Akron, OH
10 July: Alpine Valley Music Theatre, East Troy, WI

CANADA
12 July: Canadian National Exhibition Grandstand, Toronto
14 July: Colisée Pepsi, Quebec City
15 July: Ottawa Civic Centre

USA
18 July: Pittsburgh Civic Arena, PA
23 July: Hersheypark Arena, Hershey, PA
24 July: Coliseum, Largo, MD
25 July: Park Amphitheatre, Erie, PA
27, 28 & 29 July: Great Woods Performing Arts Center, Mansfield, MA
1, 2 & 3 August: Madison Square Garden, NYC
6 & 7 August: East Rutherford – Brendan Byrne Arena, NJ
9 & 10 August: Uniondale – Nassau Veterans Memorial Coliseum, NY

AUSTRALIA
5, 6,7,8,9 & 10 September: Melbourne Sports and Entertainment Centre, Victoria
12 September: Brisbane Entertainment Centre, Queensland
14, 15, 16, 17 & 18 September: Sydney – Sydney Entertainment Centre, New South Wales

NEW ZEALAND
19 September: Western Springs, Auckland, North Island

JAPAN
24, 25, 26, 27, 28, 29 & 30 September: Nippon Budokan, Tokyo
1 October: Yokohama Cultural Gymnasium
3, 5 & 6 October: Osaka-jo Hall
7 October: Shizuoko Industrial Hall

USA
15,16 & 17 October: Neal S. Blaisdell Center, Honolulu, HI

THE *SLIPPERY WHEN WET* TOUR DATES 1986–1987

FESTIVALS
4 July 1986: Farm Aid 2, Manor Downs, Austin, TX
30 August 1986: Monsters Of Rock, Zeppelinfled, Nuremberg, Germany
31 August 1986: Monsters Of Rock, Maimarkt-Gelande, Mannheim, Germany
22 August 1987: Monsters Of Rock, Donington Park, England

SELECTIVE DISCOGRAPHY
Slippery When Wet

The following discography covers the original release as well as subsequent reissues and multimedia releases relating to the album ...

ALBUMS
USA/UK Original Release, (Mercury, 1986)
Formats: CD, LP, Cassette
Tracklisting: Let It Rock/ You Give Love A Bad Name/Livin' On A Prayer/Social Disease/Wanted Dead Or Alive/Raise Your Hands/Without Love/I'd Die For You/Never Say Goodbye/Wild In The Streets

Collector's Edition Picture Disc (Vertigo, 1986)
Tracklisting: Let It Rock/ You Give Love A Bad Name/Livin' On A Prayer/Social Disease/Wanted Dead Or Alive/Raise Your Hands/Without Love/I'd Die For You/Never Say Goodbye/Wild In The Streets
Please note, the US and UK versions have different pictures

Japanese Reissue (Mercury, 1998)
Format: 2 CDs
Tracklisting: Let It Rock/ You Give Love A Bad Name/Livin' On A Prayer/Social Disease/Wanted Dead Or Alive/Raise Your Hands/Without Love/I'd Die For You/Never Say Goodbye/Wild In The Streets
Bonus CD: Wanted Dead Or Alive (*Live; Wembley, 1995*)/Livin' On A Prayer (*Live; USA, 1987*)/You Give Love A Bad Name (*Live; USA, 1987*)/Wild In The Streets (*Live; Wembley, 1995*)/Borderline (*Studio Outtake*)/Edge Of A Broken Heart (*Studio Outtake*)/Never Say Goodbye (*Live Acoustic Version*)

LET IT ROCK

DualDisc Reissue (Mercury, 2005)
Formats: CD, DVD
Tracklisting: Let It Rock/ You Give Love A Bad Name/Livin' On A Prayer/Social Disease/Wanted Dead Or Alive/Raise Your Hands/Without Love/I'd Die For You/Never Say Goodbye/Wild In The Streets
DVD: You Give Love A Bad Name (*Promo Video*)/Livin' On A Prayer (*Promo Video*)/Wanted Dead Or Alive (*Promo Video*)/Never Say Goodbye (*Promo Video*)/ I'd Die For You/Never Say Goodbye (*Promo Video*)

NOTE: *The DVD also contained an expanded audio version of the album with additional aspects to the songs thus adding to their running times.*

Special Edition Reissue (Mercury, 2010)
Format: CD
Tracklisting: Let It Rock/ You Give Love A Bad Name/Livin' On A Prayer/Social Disease/Wanted Dead Or Alive/Raise Your Hands/Without Love/I'd Die For You/Never Say Goodbye/Wild In The Streets
Bonus Tracks: You Give Love A Bad Name (*Live; USA, 1987*)/ Livin' On A Prayer (*Live; 1987*)/ Wanted Dead Or Alive (*Live Acoustic Version*)

SINGLES

You Give Love A Bad Name (7"/CD) (Mercury, 1986)
Extra Tracks: Raise Your Hands/Let It Rock

Livin' On A Prayer (7"/12"/CD (Mercury, 1986)
Extra Tracks: Wild In The Streets/Edge Of A Broken Heart

Wanted Dead Or Alive (7"/CD) (Mercury, 1987)
Extra Tracks: Never Say Goodbye/I'd Die For You

Wanted Dead Or Alive (7" Promo) (Mercury, 1987)
Extra Tracks: Wanted Dead Or Alive (Short Version)

Wanted Dead Or Alive (Japanese 7") (Mercury, 1987)
Extra Tracks: Shot Through The Heart

Wanted Dead Or Alive (Japanese CD Maxi) (Mercury, 1987)
Extra Tracks: Wanted Dead Or Alive (*Acoustic*)/Wanted Dead Or Alive (*Live*)/ Edge Of A Broken Heart

SELECTIVE DISCOGRAPHY

Wanted Dead Or Alive (CD Single) (Mercury, 2001)
Extra Tracks: Wanted Dead Or Alive (*Live, Radio Edit*)/Wanted Dead Or Alive (*Live, Acoustic*)/Next 100 Years (Live)/Not Fade Away (*Live, JBJ Solo*)

Wanted Dead Or Alive (CD Video) (Mercury, 2003)
Extra Tracks: Never Say Goodbye/I'd Die For You/Wanted Dead Or Alive (*Acoustic*)/Wanted Dead Or Alive (*Promo Video*)

Wanted Dead Or Alive (CD Single), (Mercury, 2003)
Extra Tracks: Wanted Dead Or Alive (Live)/Thank You For Loving Me (*Live*)

Wanted Dead Or Alive (Limited Edition CD Promo) (Mercury, 2003)
B-sides: Wanted Dead Or Alive (*Live*)/The Distance (*Live*)

Never Say Goodbye (7"/CD) (Mercury, 1987)
Extra Tracks: Never Say Goodbye/Edge Of A Broken Heart (*USA*); Never Say Goodbye/Shot Through The Heart (*Live*) (*Euro*)

Never Say Goodbye (UK/USA Re-release; CD) (Mercury, 1987)
Extra Tracks: Social Disease/Edge Of A Broken Heart/Raise Your Hands

OTHER SINGLES
Borderline *(An EP released in Japan in 1986)*
Let It Rock *(12" promo LP released in the UK in 1986)*
Edge Of A Broken Heart *(Never released as a physical single; it featured on the* Disorderlies *soundtrack and was released to radio in 1987.)*

VHS
Slippery When Wet: The Videos (Mercury, 1987)
Tracklisting: Wild In The Streets/Livin' On A Prayer (*Live at MTV Awards 1987*)/You Give Love A Bad Name/Never Say Goodbye/Livin' On A Prayer/Wanted Dead Or Alive

PROMO VIDEOS
You Give Love A Bad Name (1986)
Dir. by Wayne Isham

Livin' On A Prayer (1986)
Dir. by Wayne Isham

LET IT ROCK

Wanted Dead Or Alive (1987)
Dir. by Wayne Isham

Never Say Goodbye (1987)
Dir. by Wayne Isham

Wild In The Streets (1987)
Dir. by Wayne Isham

Wanted Dead Or Alive (2003)
Dir. by Anthony M. Bongiovi

**SELECTIVE DISCOGRAPHY
BON JOVI**

Here is a fairly extensive, albeit selected, Bon Jovi discography. Though *Slippery When Wet* and its various releases have already been covered in this book I have elected to include a full back catalogue discography of the band as well as selected solo releases of JBJ, Richie Sambora and David Bryan for your reference ...

**STUDIO ALBUMS
BON JOVI** (Mercury, 1984)
Tracklisting: Runaway/Roulette/She Don't Know Me/Shot Through The Heart/ Love Lies/Breakout/Burning For Love/Come Back/Get Ready

7800° FAHRENHEIT (Mercury, 1985)
Tracklisting: In And Out Of Love/The Price Of Love/Only Lonely/King Of The Mountain/Silent Night/Tokyo Road/The Hardest Part Is The Night/Always Run To You/(I Don't Wanna Fall) To The Fire/Secret Dreams/In And Out Of Love*
*Live CD video on the remastered version

SLIPPERY WHEN WET (Mercury, 1986)
Tracklisting: Let It Rock/ You Give Love A Bad Name/Livin' On A Prayer/Social Disease/Wanted Dead Or Alive/Raise Your Hands/Without Love/I'd Die For You/Never Say Goodbye/Wild In The Streets/Wanted Dead Or Alive*
*Live CD video on the remastered version

NEW JERSEY (Mercury, 1988)
Tracklisting: Lay Your Hands On Me/Bad Medicine/Born To Be My Baby/Living In Sin/Blood On Blood/Homebound Train/Wild Is The Wind/Ride Cowboy Ride/

SELECTIVE DISCOGRAPHY

Stick To Your Guns/I'll Be There For You/99 In The Shade/Love For Sale/Lay Your Hands On Me*
*Live CD video on the remastered version

KEEP THE FAITH (Mercury, 1992)
Tracklisting: I Believe/Keep The Faith/I'll Sleep When I'm Dead/In These Arms/Bed Of Roses/If I Was Your Mother/Dry County/Woman In Love/Fear/I Want You/Blame It On The Love Of Rock & Roll/Little Bit Of Soul/Keep The Faith*
*Live CD video on the remastered version

THESE DAYS (Mercury, 1995)
Tracklisting: Hey God/Something For The Pain/This Ain't A Love Song/These Days/Lie To Me/Damned/My Guitar Lies Bleeding In My Arms/(It's Hard) Letting You Go/Hearts Breaking Even/Something To Believe In/If That's What It Takes/Diamond Ring/All I Want Is Everything/Bitter Wine

CRUSH (Island, 2000)
Tracklisting: It's My Life/Say It Isn't So/Thank You For Loving Me/Two Story Town/Next 100 Years/Just Older/Mystery Train/Save The World/Captain Crash & The Beauty Queen From Mars/She's A Mystery/I Got The Girl/One Wild Night/I Could Make A Living Out Of Lovin' You*/It's My Life+/Say It Isn't So
*Demo bonus track
+ Remix bonus track

BOUNCE (Island, 2002)
Tracklisting: Undivided/Everyday/The Distance/Joey/Misunderstood/All About Lovin' You/Hook Me Up/Right Side Of Wrong/Love Me Back To Life/You Had Me From Hello/Bounce/Open All Night
(NB: This release includes exclusive bonus video footage)

HAVE A NICE DAY (Island, 2005)
Tracklisting: Have A Nice Day/I Want To Be Loved/Welcome To Wherever You Are/Who Says You Can't Go Home/Last Man Standing/Bells Of Freedom/Wildflower/Last Cigarette/I Am/Complicated/Novocaine/Story Of My Life/Dirty Little Secret*/Unbreakable*
*Bonus tracks

LOST HIGHWAY (Mercury Nashville, 2007)
Tracklisting: Lost Highway/Summertime/(You Want To) Make A Memory/

LET IT ROCK

Whole Lot Of Leavin'/We Got It Going On/Any Other Day/Seat Next To You/ Everybody's Broken/Till We Ain't Strangers Anymore (featuring LeAnn Rimes)/ The Last Night/One Step Closer/I Love This Town/Lonely

THE CIRCLE (Island, 2009)
Tracklisting: We Weren't Born To Follow/When We Were Beautiful/Work For The Working Man/Superman Tonight/Bullet/Thorn In My Side/Live Before You Die/ Brokenpromiseland/Love's The Only Rule/Fast Cars/Happy Now/Learn To Love

WHAT ABOUT NOW (Island, 2013)
Tracklisting: Because We Can/I'm With You/What About Now/Pictures Of You/ Amen/That's What The Water Made Me/What's Left Of Me/Army Of One/Thick As Thieves/The Beautiful World/Room At The End Of The World/The Fighter/ These Two Hands*/Not Running Anymore*/Old Habits Die Hard*/Every Road Leads Home To You*

RARE ALBUMS & EPs
Live On Tour EP (1987) (EP)
Hard & Hot (1991)
Keep The Faith – Live (1993)
These Days – Special Edition (1996)
Live From Osaka (2000) (EP)
The Love Songs (2001) (EP)
Tokyo Road – Best Of Bon Jovi (2001)
Bon Jovi – Target EP (2003) (EP)
Cross Road – Deluxe Sound + Vision (2005)
Live From The Have A Nice Day Tour (2005) (*Walmart only released promo*)
Lost Highway – The Concert (2007)

COMPILATIONS
CROSS ROAD: THE GREATEST HITS (Mercury, 1994)
Tracklisting: Livin' On A Prayer/Keep The Faith/Someday I'll Be Saturday Night/ Always/Wanted Dead Or Alive/Lay Your Hands On Me/You Give Love A Bad Name/Bed Of Roses/Blaze Of Glory/In These Arms/ Bad Medicine/I'll Be There For You/In And Out Of Love/Runaway/Never Say Goodbye

SELECTIVE DISCOGRAPHY

THIS LEFT FEELS RIGHT (Island, 2003)
Tracklisting: Wanted Dead Or Alive/Livin' On A Prayer/Bad Medicine/It's My Life/Lay Your Hands On Me/You Give Love A Bad Name/Bed Of Roses/Everyday/Born To Be My Baby/Keep The Faith/I'll Be There For You/Always/The Distance*/Joey*
*Bonus live tracks

100,000,000 BON JOVI FANS CAN'T BE WRONG (Island, 2004)
Tracklisting: (*Disc 1*) Why Aren't You Dead?/The Radio Saved My Life Tonight/Taking It Back/Someday I'll Be Saturday Night*/Miss Fourth Of July/Open All Night/These Arms Are Open All Night/I Get A Rush/Someday Just Might Be Tonight/Thief Of Hearts/Last Man Standing/I Just Want To Be Your Man
*Demo
(*Disc 2*) Garageland/Starting All Over Again/Maybe Someday/Last Chance Train/The Fire Inside/Every Beat Of My Heart/Rich Man Living In A Poor Man's House/The One That Got Away/You Can Sleep While I Dream/Outlaws Of Love/Good Guys Don't Always Wear White/We Rule The Night
(*Disc 3*) Edge Of A Broken Heart/Sympathy/Only In My Dreams*/Shut Up And Kiss Me/Crazy Love/Lonely At The Top/Ordinary People/Flesh And Bone/Satellite/If I Can't Have Your Love+/Real Life/Memphis Lives In Me#/Too Much Of A Good Thing
* Feat. Tico Torres on vocals
+ Feat. Richie Sambora on vocals
# Feat. David Bryan on vocals from the musical Memphis
(*Disc 4*) Love Ain't Nothing But A Four Letter Word/Love Ain't Nothing But A Four Letter Word*/River Runs Dry/Always*/Kidnap An Angel/Breathe/Out Of Bounds/Letter To A Friend/Temptation/Gotta Have A Reason/All I Wanna Do Is You/Billy/Nobody's Hero*/Livin' On A Prayer+
* Demo
+ Previously unreleased, hidden track
(NB: Discs 1-3 are collections of previously unreleased tracks, B-sides, demos, soundtrack compositions and obscurities. The fourth disc is a DVD of interviews and archive footage.)

GREATEST HITS (Island, 2010) (US)
Tracklisting: (*CD 1*) Livin' On A Prayer/You Give Love A Bad Name/It's My Life/Have A Nice Day/Wanted Dead Or Alive/Bad Medicine/We Weren't Born To

LET IT ROCK

Follow/I'll Be There For You/Born To Be My Baby/Blaze Of Glory/Who Says You Can't Go Home (*with Jennifer Nettles*)/Lay Your Hands On Me/Always/ Runaway/What Do You Got?/No Apologies/ Diamond Ring (live)*/We Weren't Born To Follow (live)*
(*CD2*) In These Arms/Someday I'll Be Saturday Night/Lost Highway/Keep The Faith/When We Were Beautiful/Bed Of Roses/This Ain't A Love Song/These Days/(You Want To)/ Make A Memory/Blood On Blood/This Is Love, This Is Life/The More Things Change
*Bonus Tracks on the Target Corporation edition
(NB: The 'Ultimate Collection' is two discs rather than the standard retail version which is a single disc ...)

GREATEST HITS (Island, 2010) (International)
Tracklisting: (CD1) Livin' On A Prayer/You Give Love A Bad Name/It's My Life/ Have A Nice Day/Wanted Dead Or Alive/Bad Medicine/We Weren't Born To Follow/I'll Be There For You/Born To Be My Baby/Who Says You Can't Go Home/Lay Your Hands On Me/Always/In These Arms/What Do You Got?/ No Apologies/Tokyo Road*
(*CD 2*) Runaway/Someday I'll Be Saturday Night/Lost Highway/I'll Sleep When I'm Dead/In And Out Of Love/Keep The Faith/When We Were Beautiful/Blaze of Glory/This Ain't A Love Song/These Days/(You Want To) Make A Memory/Blood On Blood/This Is Love, This Is Life/The More Things Change/This Is Our House*
*Bonus track on the Japanese version on Disc 1
* Bonus track on iTunes version on Disc 2

LIVE ALBUMS
ONE WILD NIGHT LIVE: 1985–2001 (Island, 2001)
Tracklisting: It's My Life (*Recorded: 27 November 2000 in Toronto, Ontario, Canada*)/Livin' On A Prayer (*Recorded: 30 August 2000 in Zurich, Switzerland*)/ You Give Love A Bad Name (*Recorded: 30 August 2000 in Zurich, Switzerland*)/ Keep The Faith (*Recorded: 20 September 2000 in New York City, USA*)/Someday I'll Be Saturday Night (*Recorded: 10 November 1995 in Melbourne, Australia*)/ Rockin' In The Free World (*Recorded: 1 December 1995 in Johannesburg, South Africa*)/Something To Believe In (*Recorded:19 May 1996 in Yokohama, Japan*)/ Wanted Dead Or Alive (*Recorded: 20 September 2000 in New York City, USA*)/Runaway(*Recorded: 28 April 1985 in Tokyo, Japan*)/In And Out Of Love(*Recorded: 28 April 1985 in Tokyo, Japan*)/I Don't Like Mondays*

SELECTIVE DISCOGRAPHY

(*Recorded: 25 June 1995 at Wembley Stadium, London, England*)/Just Older (*Recorded: 27 November 2000 in Toronto, Ontario, Canada*) /Something For The Pain(*Recorded: 10 November 1995 in Melbourne, Australia*)/Bad Medicine(*Recorded: 30 August 2000 in Zurich, Switzerland*)/One Wild Night 2001+ (*Recorded: 27 November 2000 in Toronto, Ontario, Canada*)
*With Bob Geldof   +Remix

INSIDE OUT (Island, 2012; Download)
Tracklisting: Blood On Blood/Lost Highway/Born To Be My Baby/You Give Love A Bad Name/Whole Lot Of Leavin'/Raise Your Hands/We Got It Going On/ Have A Nice Day/It's My Life/I'll Be There For You/We Weren't Born To Follow/Wanted Dead Or Alive/Livin' On A Prayer/Keep The Faith

SINGLES

"Runaway" (1983)
"She Don't Know Me" (1984)
"Burning For Love" (1984)
"Only Lonely" (1985)
"In And Out Of Love" (1985)
"The Hardest Part Is The Night" (1985)
"You Give Love A Bad Name" (1986)
"Livin' On A Prayer" (1986)
'Wanted Dead Or Alive' (1987)
"Never Say Goodbye" (1987)
"Bad Medicine" (1988)
"Born To Be My Baby" (1988)
"I'll Be There For You" (1989)
"Lay Your Hands On Me" (1989)
"Living In Sin" (1989)
"Keep The Faith" (1992)
"Bed Of Roses" (1993)
"In These Arms" (1993)
"I'll Sleep When I'm Dead" (1993)
"I Believe" (1993)
"Dry County" (1994)
"Always" (1994)
"Please Come Home For Christmas" (1994)

LET IT ROCK

"Someday I'll Be Saturday Night" (1995)
"This Ain't A Love Song" (1995)
"Something For The Pain" (1995)
"Lie To Me" (1995)
"These Days" (1996)
"Hey God" (1996)
"Real Life" (1999)
"It's My Life" (2000)
"Say It Isn't So" (2000)
"Thank You For Loving Me" (2000)
"One Wild Night" (2001)
"Everyday" (2002)
"Misunderstood" (2002)
"All About Lovin' You" (2003)
"Have A Nice Day" (2005)
"Who Says You Can't Go Home" (2006)
"Welcome To Wherever You Are" (2006)
"(You Want To) Make A Memory" (2007)
"Lost Highway" (2007)
"Whole Lotta Leavin'" (2008)
"We Weren't Born To Follow" (2009)
"Superman Tonight" (2010)
"When We Were Beautiful" (2010)
"What Do You Got?" (2010)
"No Apologies" (2011)
"This Is Our House" (2011)
"Because We Can" (2011)

OTHER SINGLES
(Mostly US airplay or singles released in selected countries)
"Borderline" (1986)
"Let It Rock" (1986)
"Edge Of A Broken Heart" (1987)
"I Wish It Could Be Christmas Everyday" (1992)
"Cama De Rosas" (1993)
"Good Guys Don't Always Wear White" (1994)

SELECTIVE DISCOGRAPHY

"Wedding Day" (1995)
"Como Yo Nadie Te Ha Amado" (1995)
"Tokyo Road" (Live) (2001)
"Wanted Dead Or Alive" (2003)
"Keep The Faith" (2003)
"The Radio Saved My Life Tonight" (2004)
"I Want To Be Loved" (2005)
"Summertime" (2007)
"Hallelujah" (2008)
"The More Things Change" (2011)

MUSIC VIDEOS

Runaway (1984)
Dir: Michael Cuesta

She Don't Know (1984)
Dir: Martin Kahan

In And Out Of Love (1985)
Dir: Martin Kahan

Only The Lonely (1985)
Dir: Jack Cole

Silent Night (1985)
Dir: Marcelo Epstein

You Give Love A Bad Name (1986)
Dir: Wayne Isham

Livin' On A Prayer (1986)
Dir: Wayne Isham

Wanted Dead Or Alive (1987)
Dir: Wayne Isham

Never Say Goodbye (1987)
Dir: Wayne Isham

Wild In The Streets (1987)
Dir: Wayne Isham

Bad Medicine (1988)
Dir Wayne Isham

Born To Be My Baby (1988)
Dir: Wayne Isham

I'll Be There For You (1989)
Dir: Wayne Isham

Lay Your Hands On Me (1989)
Dir: Wayne Isham

Living In Sin (1989)
Dir: Wayne Isham

Blood On Blood (1989)
Dir: Wayne Isham

Keep The Faith (1992)
Dir: Phil Joanou

Bed Of Roses (1993)
Dir: Wayne Isham

LET IT ROCK

In These Arms (1993)
Dir: Wayne Isham

I'll Sleep When I'm Dead (1993)
Dir: Troy Smith

I Believe (1993)
Dir: Nick Egan

If I Was Your Mother (1994)
Dir: Wayne Isham

Dry County (1994)
Dir: Nick Egan

Always (1994)
Dir: Marty Callner

Please Come Home For Christmas (1994)
Dir: Herb Ritts

Someday I'll Be Saturday Night (1994)
Dir: Wayne Isham

Good Guys Don't Always Wear White (1995)
Dir: Wayne Isham

This Ain't A Love Song (1995)
Dir: Andy Morahan

Something For The Pain (1995)
Dir: Marty Callner

Lie To Me (1995)
Dir: Marty Callner

These Days (1996)
Dir: Steven Kirlys

Hey God (1996)
Dir: Matt Mahurin

Real Life (1999)
Dir: Wayne Isham

It's My Life (2000)
Dir: Wayne Isham

Say It Isn't So (2000)
Dir: Wayne Isham

Thank You For Loving Me (2000)
Dir: Wayne Isham

One Wild Night (2001)
Dir: Nancy Bardawil

Everyday (2002)
Dir: Joseph Kahn

Misunderstood (2002)
Dir: Marc Klasfeld

All About Lovin' You (2003)
Dir: Marc Klasfeld

Wanted Dead Or Alive 2003 (2003)
Dir: Anthony M. Bongiovi

Have A Nice Day (2005)
Dir: Eric Hirschberg

Who Says You Can't Go Home (2005)
Dir: Jeff Labbe

Who Says You Can't Go Home (with Jennifer Nettles) (2005)
Dir: Anthony M. Bongiovi

SELECTIVE DISCOGRAPHY

(You Want To) Make A Memory (2006)
Dir: Kevin Kerslake

Till We Ain't Strangers Anymore (2007)
Dir: Phil Griffin

Lost Highway (2007)
Dir: Anthony M. Bongiovi

Whole Lot Of Leavin' (2008)
Dir: Phil Griffin

We Weren't Born To Follow (2009)
Dir: Craig Barry

Superman Tonight (2010)
Dir: Phil Griffin

When We Were Beautiful (2010)
Dir: Anthony M. Bongiovi

What Do You Got? (2010)
Dir: Wayne Isham

This Is Our House (2010)
Dir: Anthony M. Bongiovi

No Apologies (2011)
Dir: Anthony M. Bongiovi

Because We Can (2013)
Dir: Fisher Stevens

SELECTIVE FILMOGRAPHY

VHS
Breakout: Video Singles (1985)
Slippery When Wet: The Videos (1987)
New Jersey: The Videos (1989)
Access All Areas: A Rock & Roll Odyssey (1990)
Keep The Faith: An Evening With Bon Jovi (1993)
Keep The Faith: The Videos (1993)
Cross Road: The Videos (1994)

DVD
Live From London (1995 – VHS & DVD)
The Crush Tour (2000 – VHS & DVD)
This Left Feels Right (2003)
Live From Atlantic City (2004)
Lost Highway: The Concert (2007)
When We Were Beautiful (2009)
Live At Madison Square Garden (2009)
Greatest Hits – The Ultimate Video Collection (2010)

LET IT ROCK

BON JOVI TOURS
Bon Jovi Tour (1984)
7800° Fahrenheit Tour (1985)
Slippery When Wet Tour (1986-1987)
New Jersey Syndicate Tour (1988-1990)
Keep The Faith Tour (1993)
I'll Sleep When I'm Dead Tour (1993)
Crossroad Promo Tour (1994)
These Days Tour (1995-1996)
Crush Tour (2000)
One Wild Night Tour (2001)
Bounce Tour (2002-2003)
Have A Nice Day Tour (2005-2006)
Lost Highway Tour (2007-2008)
The Circle Tour (2010)
Bon Jovi Live (2011)
Because We Can - The Tour (2013-2014)

SELECTIVE DISCOGRAPHY
SOLO WORK

JON BON JOVI
STUDIO ALBUMS

BLAZE OF GLORY (Vertigo, 1990)
Tracklisting: Billy Get Your Guns/Miracle/Blaze Of Glory/Blood Money/Santa Fe/Justice In The Barrel/Never Say Die/You Really Got Me Now/Bang A Drum/Dyin' Ain't Much Of A Livin'/Guano City

DESTINATION ANYWHERE (PolyGram, 1997)
Tracklisting: Queen Of New Orleans/Janie, Don't Take Your Love To Town/Midnight In Chelsea/Ugly/Staring At Your Window With A Suitcase In My Hand/Every Word Was A Piece Of My Heart/It's Just Me/Destination Anywhere/Learning How To Fall/Naked/Little City/August 7/Cold Hard Heart*
*Demo version

SELECTIVE DISCOGRAPHY

THE POWER STATION YEARS: 1980-1983 (Masquerade Music, 1997)
Tracklisting: Who Said It Would Last Forever/Open Your Heart/Stringin' A Line/ Don't Leave Me Tonight/More Than We Bargained For/For You/Hollywood Dreams/All Talk, No Action/Don't Keep Me Wondering/Head Over Heels/No One Does It Like You/What You Want/Don't You Believe Him/Talkin' In Your Sleep
(NB: This was not authorized by the Bon Jovi management)

SINGLES
"Blaze Of Glory" (1990)
"Miracle" (1990)
"Midnight In Chelsea" (1997)
"Queen Of New Orleans" (1997)
"Jamie, Don't Take Your Love To Town" (1997)

FILMOGRAPHY
Destination Anywhere: The Film (1997 - VHS & DVD)

RICHIE SAMBORA
STUDIO ALBUMS

Shark Frenzy (Band)
SHARK FRENZY - VOLUME 1: 1978 (Castle/Sanctuary, 2004)
Tracklisting: Come Saturday Night/Live Fast, Love Hard, Die Young/Law Of The Jungle/Nobody/The Ones With Angel's Eye's/The Power/I'll Play The Fool/ Laura's Birthday/Southern Belle/Don't Stop Loving Me Now

(Solo)
STRANGER IN THIS TOWN (Mercury, 1991)
Tracklisting: Rest In Peace/Church Of Desire/Stranger In This Town/Ballad Of Youth/One Light Burning/Mr. Bluesman/Rosie/River Of Love/Father Time/The Answer/The Wind Cries Mary*
*Not available on every release

UNDISCOVERED SOUL (Mercury, 1998)
Tracklisting: Made In America/Hard Times Come Easy/Fallen From Graceland/ If God Was A Woman/All That Really Matters/You're Not Alone/In It For Love/ Chained/Harlem Rain/Who I Am/Downside Of Love/Undiscovered Soul

AFTERMATH OF THE LOWDOWN (Dangerbird, 2012)
Tracklisting: Burn The Candle/Every Road Leads Home To You/Taking A Chance On The Wind/Nowadays/Weathering The Storm/Sugar Daddy/I'll Always Walk Beside You/Seven Years Gone/Learning How To Fly With A Broken Wing/You Can Only Get So High/Backseat Driver*/World
*Bonus track on the Japanese version

SINGLES
"Ballad Of Youth" (1991)
"Hard Times Come Easy" (1998)
"In It For Love" (1998)

DAVID BRYAN
STUDIO ALBUMS

ON A FULL MOON (Ignition, 1995)
Tracklisting: Awakening/In These Arms/It's A Long Road/April/Kissed By An Angel/Endless Horizon/Lullaby For Two Moons/Interlude/Midnight Voodoo/Room Full Of Blues/Hear Our Prayer/Summer Of Dreams/Up The River/Netherworld Waltz

LUNAR ECLIPSE (Rounder/Moon Junction Music, 2000)
Tracklisting: Second Chance/I Can Love/It's A Long Road/On A Full Moon/April/Kissed By An Angel/Endless Horizon/Lullaby For Two Moons/Interlude/Room Full Of Blues/Hear Our Prayer/Summer Of Dreams/Up The River/Netherworld Waltz/In These Arms

AFTERWORD
BY DEREK SHULMAN

After the difficulties and mixed results of *7800° Fahrenheit*, John, Doc and myself were determined to make sure the third album was the "real deal". The band had toured extensively for three years almost without a break and had built a very strong following worldwide. The only missing ingredient for Bon Jovi's ultimate success was a huge hit album.

I broached with Jon the subject of having someone come in and co-write with him and Ritchie with trepidation. Jon, always the pragmatist, agreed to consider this option.

At the time I was working with KISS and their album *Lick It Up* was doing extremely well.

I noticed the name "Child" as a co-writer on a couple of the stronger songs and called Gene Simmons to ask who this "Child" person was. He asked if I remembered the band Desmond Child and Rouge, which I knew from my Capitol days in my band Gentle Giant. Gene told me this guy was a great writer and that I should definitely consider him to do other projects. After meeting him and agreeing with Gene's assessment, I asked Jon and Ritchie to meet and see what could come out of this pairing.

At the same time, I was becoming aware of some amazing productions coming out of a studio called Little Mountain in Vancouver, Canada. Bruce Fairbairn had produced several excellent sounding albums with his engineer Bob Rock in Canada. I had an instinct that Bruce might just be the right producer for Bon Jovi's third album. We all met and the chemistry was perfect. For whatever reason, it seemed the stars were aligned and when I heard the initial demos I knew my instincts were right.

LET IT ROCK

Bruce, Bob, Doc and myself and the band holed up in Vancouver for several weeks and when the final mixes were complete it was obvious to all who heard this album that this was indeed something very "special". The groundwork had been laid with the incredible touring the band had done and the comparative success of the two previous albums.

The only glitch in setting up this album was the artwork which was trashed at the eleventh hour and Jon came to the company with a black plastic garbage bag, sprayed water on it and wrote "*Slippery When Wet*" with his finger. The company had readied the marketing plan for the band, the tour had been set up by Doc and the single "You Give Love A Bad Name" was released with a big budget video for MTV. The reaction to the single and album was instantaneous. It became obvious that this was going to be a landmark album for the band.

Little did we know that almost 30 years later the songs and the band would remain as popular now as they were in 1986.

Derek Shulman
(Former Senior Vice President of PolyGram Records)

BIBLIOGRAPHY & FURTHER READING

Most of the following books are out of print but you should be able to purchase secondhand copies on Amazon or eBay, if you look hard enough ...

BOOKS

Bateman, Bill. *Bon Jovi.* (Music Book Services, 1996)
Bowler, Dave & Bryan Dray. *Bon Jovi: Runaway.* (Boxtree Ltd, 1996)
Daniels, Neil. *Bon Jovi Encyclopaedia.* (Chrome Dreams, 2009)
Heatley, Michael. *Bon Jovi: In Their Own Words.* (Omnibus Press, 1997)
Heatley, Michael. *Jon Bon Jovi.* (Omnibus Press, 1998)
Jackson, Laura. *Jon Bon Jovi: The Biography.* (Portrait, 2003)
Jan, Ramona. *Bon Jovi.* (Paperjacks, 1988)
Jeffries, Neil. *Bon Jovi.* (Sidgwick & Jackson Ltd, 1996)
Kamin, Philip & Greg Quill. *Bon Jovi: Hard Rock Of The 80s.* (Philip Kamin Publishing Inc., 1987)
McSquare, Eddie. *Bon Jovi: An Illustrated Biography.* (Omnibus Press, 1990)
St. Michael, Mick. *Bon Jovi.* (Omnibus Press, 1988)
Wall, Mick & Malcolm Dome. *Bon Jovi: All Night Long* (Omnibus Press, 1995)
Wall, Mick & Malcolm Dome. *Bon Jovi: Live!* (Omnibus Press, 1996)
Wall, Mick & Malcolm Dome. *The Complete Guide To The Music Of Bon Jovi.* (Omnibus Press, 1996)

WEBSITES
http://www.bonjovi.com
http://www.myspace.com/bonjovi
http://www.facebook.com/BonJovi
http://www.backstagejbj.com
http://www.davidbryan.com
http://www.Tico-Torres.com
http://www.ticoshow.com
http://www.hueymcdonald.com

SOURCES

The following publications and websites were integral
in writing this book ...

BOOKS

Betts, Graham. *Complete UK Hit Singles 1952-2005.* (London: Collins, 2005)
Betts, Graham. *Complete UK Hit Albums: 1956-2005.* (London: Collins, 2005)
Friend, Lonn. *Life On Planet Rock.* (Portrait, 2006)
Larkin, Colin. *The Virgin Encyclopaedia Of Rock.* (Virgin Books, 1999)
Roberts, David (Ed.) *British Hit Singles & Albums (19th Edition.)* (Guinness World Records Ltd, 2006)
Strong, Martin C. *The Great Rock Discography. (6th Edition)* (London: Canongate, 2002)
Wall, Mick. *Star Trippin': The Best Of Mick Wall 1985-91* (M&G, 2006)

MUSIC MAGAZINES

Classic Rock
Fireworks
Hard Roxx
Kerrang!
Metal Attack
Metal Edge
Metal Forces
Metal Hammer
NME
Powerplay
RAW
Request
Rolling Stone
SPIN
Total Guitar

MAGAZINES & NEWSPAPERS

Daily Record
Glamour Magazine
Huffington Post
Interview Magazine
The Guardian

WEBSITES

http://www.allmusic.com
http://www.antimusic.com
http://www.artistdirect.com
http://www.artistwd.com/joyzine
http://www.billboard.com
http://www.bravewords.com
http://www.cdnow.com
http://www.classicrockmagazine.com

http://www.classicrockrevisited.com
http://www.dailyrecord.co.uk
http://www.getreadytorock.com
http://www.guitarworld.com
http://www.huffingtonpost.com
http://www.melodicrock.com
http://www.musicradar.com
http://www.rocktopia.co.uk
http://www.rockunited.com
http://www.rollingstone.com
http://www.soundonsound.com
http://www.timeout.com
http://www.ultimate-guitar.com
http://www.VH-1.com

ACKNOWLEDGEMENTS

A big thank you to the following rockers and rollers for help with this book: Lesley Aeschliman/Phil Ashcroft/Ron Boudreau/Bailey Brothers/Steve Blaze/ Jerry Bloom/Joe Bosso/Jake Brown/Ray Brown/ John Carucci/Andreas Carlsson/ Mónica Castedo-López/Robert Christgau/Roy Davis/Robert Dimery/Don Dokken/Malcolm Dome/Paul Elliot/Rob Evans/Robert Fleischman/Ian Fortnam/ Tony Franklin/ Phil & Sue Godsell/Jimmy Guterman/Elianne Halbersberg/Ross Halfin/Neil Jeffries/Pete Jupp/Holly Knight /Bruce Kulick/Mitch Lafon/Andrew Leahey/Tommy Mandel/Joe Matera/Alan McGee/Jason McMaster/Bruce Mee/Kas Mercer /Tony Mills/Tom Marolda/Derek Oliver/ Glenn O'Brien/ Ian Parry/Dean Pedley/Ricky Phillips/Anne Raso/Jason Ritchie/Steven Rosen/Dave Shack/Derek Shulman/Ingrid Sischy/Stuart Smith/Billy Squier/Allison Stewart/Marc Storace/ Kasim Sultan/Paul Suter/Sylvie Simmons/Caroline Sullivan/ Kimmo Toivonen/ Mike Tramp/John Tucker/Joe Lynn Turner/Jonathan Valen/Mark Weiss/Chris Welch/Ron Wikso/David Wild/ Simon Witter/Jeb Wright.

Apologies for those names that I'm bound to have forgotten!

DISCLAIMER

Thank you to the copyright holders for allowing the author to quote from the referenced sources/texts. However, it has not been possible to contact every copyright holder though great efforts were made. The author and publisher would be happy to amend/delete/credit where appropriate any sources in future editions of this work should the copyright holders get in touch. A special thank you must go to all those whose work the author has referenced and fully credited in this book. The opinions of the writers and artists quoted in this book do not necessarily represent those of the author.

ABOUT THE AUTHOR

NEIL DANIELS is the author of the acclaimed *Bon Jovi Encyclopaedia* as well as a dozen other books on rock and metal. His other titles include books on Robert Plant, Judas Priest, Linkin Park, Metallica, Iron Maiden, You Me At Six, AC/DC and Journey. He had more than ten books published between 2007 and 2014. His books have so far been translated into Polish, German, Czech, Italian, Bulgarian, Finnish, Japanese and French with several more foreign titles forthcoming. His reviews, articles and interviews on music and pop culture have been published in *The Guardian, Classic Rock Presents AOR, Classic Rock Presents Let It Rock, Rock Sound, Record Collector, Big Cheese, Powerplay, Fireworks, MediaMagazine, Rocktopia.co.uk, Get Ready To Rock.com, musicOMH.com, Drowned In Sound.com, BBCNewsOnline.co.uk, Carling.com, Unbarred.co.uk* and *Planet Sound* on Channel4's defunct Teletext service.

More information is obtainable at *www.neildanielsbooks.com*. Neil can also be found on Facebook, LinkedIn, Tumblr and Twitter.

ABOUT THE AUTHOR

PUBLISHED BOOKS BY NEIL DANIELS

The Story Of Judas Priest: Defenders Of The Faith (Omnibus Press, 2007)
Robert Plant: Led Zeppelin, Jimmy Page & The Solo Years (Independent Music Press, 2008)
Bon Jovi Encyclopaedia (Chrome Dreams, 2009)
Dawn Of The Metal Gods: My Life In Judas Priest & Heavy Metal (with Al Atkins) (Iron Pages, 2009)
Linkin Park – An Operator's Manual (Chrome Dreams, 2009)
Don't Stop Believin' – The Untold Story Of Journey (Omnibus Press, 2011)
Rock Landmarks: Judas Priest's British Steel (Wymer Publishing, 2011)
Metallica – The Early Years And The Rise Of Metal (Independent Music Press, 2012)
Iron Maiden – The Ultimate Unauthorized History Of The Beast (Voyageur Press, 2012)
You Me At Six – A Biography (Independent Music Press, 2012)
AC/DC – The Early Years With Bon Scott (Independent Music Press, 2013)
Reinventing Metal – The True Story Of Pantera And The Tragically Short Life Of Dimebag Darrell (Backbeat Books, 2013)

Soundcheck Books have also published Neil Daniels'

High Stakes And Dangerous Men: The UFO Story
(ISBN: 978-0-9571442-6 2)

Beer Drinkers And Hell Raisers: A ZZ Top Guide
(ISBN: 978-0-9571442-7-9)

Killers: The Origins Of Iron Maiden
(ISBN: 978-0-9575700-2-3)

Available from all good booksellers.